Are you a young momma—
or planning to become one?

Mother's Day Is Over
can change your life!

This painfully honest and human book tells
you what being a mother is really like. From her
own experience as a mother of two children she
loves and from interviews with other women
who know mothering first hand, Shirley Radl
gives an unvarnished job description.

She is just as frank in reporting how many
mothers feel about it. You will discover you are
not alone if you feel inadequate, fearful, resentful—even angry—at the burden of budget-
ing, the destruction of your possessions, the cost
to your marriage of the drain on your energy,
patience and appearance.

Mother's Day Is Over
offers you the solace of knowing that such feelings are normal, and support in that important
struggle to hold onto your "self" through it all.

MOTHER'S DAY is over

By SHIRLEY L. RADL

WARNER
PAPERBACK
LIBRARY

A Warner Communications Company

WARNER PAPERBACK LIBRARY EDITION
First Printing: November, 1974

Library of Congress Catalog Card Number: 72-96620

This Warner Paperback Library Edition is published by arrangement
with Charterhouse, Inc.

Warner Paperback Library is a division of Warner Books, Inc.,
75 Rockefeller Plaza, New York, N.Y. 10019.

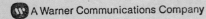 A Warner Communications Company

Printed in the United States of America

To my husband, Cal,
and our two children,
Lisa and Adam.

✿ acknowledgments

My first thanks must go to my dear friend, John R. Rague of New York. From the moment I started writing, John encouraged me to continue. When I wavered, his encouragement became stronger. When, at one point, I became discouraged, he launched an all-out offensive, writing and telephoning me so often that I felt I should write the book just to stop his nagging. A kind, loyal, and empathetic man, he inspired me with the confidence to write the book.

Joining John Rague were my friends Carol Petrick and Bob Clayton, who not only made me feel guilty when I wasn't working on the book but helped me type the early drafts. Carol's honest criticism, sometimes a dangerous thing, was an enormous help.

I must acknowledge the influence of Alicia Moore of *Life* and Mark Ross of *Environmental Quality* magazine, who both encouraged me and helped me because of their enthusiasm for the book.

And the mothers. A mother I call Sharon whose sad story and concern for other young women demonstrated a need for this book. And all of the mothers who had enough confidence in me to share their thoughts honestly with me.

I'm very grateful to a militant non-mother, Ellen Peck, who became a fine friend before we ever met—a woman who, without much ado, offered and gave help.

And my editor, Carol Eisen Rinzler, who deftly guided me, spotted the important ommissions, knew instinctively what pieces I cherished, and became a treasured friend through it all. Throughout the rewriting and editing of

Mother's Day Is Over, I've known inside that the book means as much to Carol as it does to me.

My greatest thanks must go to my husband, who not only unflinchingly encouraged me, but who was so patient with a wife who spent endless nights at the typewriter, poring over articles, or worse, when not so occupied, being physically present, but not present at all. For helping me in a million ways, from watching the kids so I could meet a deadline to just being there.

❦ foreword

For some time I have been reluctant to publish my views on motherhood. I feared that my words, born out of concern for my children's, my husband's, and my own future, might be attributed to supposedly negative feelings about my children.

But beyond that, it has been difficult to admit to myself that my beautiful, wanted, and planned children have been capable of arousing within me resentment, hostility, and rage—and that they could be a source of profound frustration and a cause of serious disturbance in my once ideal marriage. Having admitted as much, though, I feared that to reveal these deep emotions would be to risk inflicting real pain within my family—a price not worth the gamble.

I have decided to speak up because I believe that what I have to say is important—and because I believe there's enough love and understanding in our family to bear the truth as Mother sees and feels it.

My own case, I feel certain, is no isolated one, either in terms of what I feel about motherhood or my reluctance to speak up. Women's feelings about being mothers have been a closely guarded secret for many years. There is almost a conspiracy of silence surrounding motherhood; if those women now contemplating having children are to have a chance of becoming good, fulfilled mothers, they must know what the job is before blithely taking it on. If only for them, the silence should be broken.

There is another group I hope will be served in this

process: mothers—and there are a great many—who have felt unnatural, guilty, ashamed, and depressed about their real feelings toward motherhood—mothers who have wanted to ask for some sympathy and understanding but who have been afraid to. No one in our society has felt so alone, perhaps, as the mother who takes little joy in being a mother. Reading this book will, I hope, bring some comfort to such mothers who may begin to believe that they are not alone in their feelings nor are they unnatural monsters.

I did not hire Louis Harris to take a poll to support the views offered here. Nor have I interviewed legions of psychologists, counselors, or other experts. Instead, I have consulted with another kind of expert—women whose principal credential is the same as mine: experience. The women I talked with, about two hundred of them, were open with me because I'm a mother with problems and feelings similar to theirs. Most of them, I suspect, would have been a good deal more guarded with a male journalist or sociologist, or with a woman without children.

The women with whom I have talked may not be "typical" by absolute standards—I took no demographic profile of the community—nor reflect everyone's experience. But they do represent a wide spectrum of women, ranging economically from lower- to upper-middle-class. Educationally, they ranged from high school graduates to Ph.D. holders. They included childless women and women with five children. If the sample is relatively small, the consensus among them, I submit, reflects attitudes and feelings of high validity and wide relevance.

I have purposely chosen not to stack the deck by dealing extensively with the plight of economically deprived mothers whose problems truly are of tragic dimensions. Nor have I considered motherhood under exceptionally difficult circumstances. The focus here is on average mothers in average homes, with healthy children and without financial distress. The reality of these typical situations is enough, if faced and considered honestly, to cause any young woman to think twice before embarking upon motherhood.

In *The Baby Trap,* Ellen Peck dealt insightfully with

the role of the media in bringing massive pressure upon women to reproduce. Calling down those who, for their own financial gain and that of their benefactors, argue that family life is virtuous and beautiful in proportion to the size of one's family, her book demands an honest response from those of us who have experienced the realities of parenthood and the problems they present. These go far beyond the loss of sex appeal, the financial burdens of child-rearing, or even divorce. They deal with a woman's total identity and sense of self-worth—problems I hope to illustrate here. Ms. Peck has told how the baby trap is set. As one who swallowed the bait, I am going to deal with what happens after the trap is sprung.

My aim is to show that it is not enough for every child to be a wanted child, as Planned Parenthood advocates. The planned and wanted children of the world often wind up unwanted after they've been around awhile. Our job is to make as sure as we can that every child is wanted not only at the time of conception and birth but forever afterward.

SHIRLEY L. RADL
Palo Alto, California
November 1972

contents

Acknowledgments   7

Foreword   9

1. A Mother Is   17

2. Pressure to Bear   39

3. The Garden of Eden   57

4. The Joys of Parenthood   71

5. Hi, I'm Mommy. Fly Me to the Cuckoo's Nest   91

6. School Days   99

7. Molding Young Minds and Morals   123

8. Spare the Rod   139

9. Marital Bliss and Children   151

10. Wrest and Wreckreation   177

11. They Are Worth Their Weight in Gold   191

12. Doctor, Lawyer, Indian Chief . . . or Mother   205

Afterword   227

Notes   237

MOTHER'S DAY is over

1

❧ a Mother is

... *Young people don't realize that this
task—this parenthood business—is endless.
It is twenty-four hours a day seven days a
week, and there are no days off from it
because there are no days off from worry,
concern, and doubt.*

*We went into it with our eyes wide open,
and they keep opening wider with every
day of parenthood. I'm not sure that knowing
what we know now, we would have become
parents—paradoxical because, by God, you
really do love the little tykes. Maybe that's
part of the strain—you try so hard to be good
parents and because you care so deeply,
you are always aware that you are gambling
with [a child's] life. I know that my wife
feels this even more keenly, for she's with
him all day, as generally a mother is.*

—A LETTER TO THE AUTHOR FROM
A FORTY-YEAR-OLD EPISCOPALIAN MINISTER

EVERYONE KNOWS WHAT A MOTHER IS.

A mother is someone who makes you wear galoshes when it isn't raining. She gives you aspirin when you have a cold and reads you stories before bed.

A mother is a happy, warm, patient person who effortlessly maintains a beautiful, spotless home. She plays games with her children joyously, teaches them constantly, and takes them to the doctor, the dentist, the zoo, the park, swimming and camping—sometimes all on the same day.

A mother is lovely and young—there are no middle-aged mommies who look middle-aged—and always looks stunning. She is cheerful, energetic, and always interested in all aspects of her family's life.

A mother is a loving, mature person who is virtually incapable of thinking petty thoughts about anyone, least of all her own children. She harbors no resentment over being unable to read a book when she wants to, take a bath when she wants to, or make love to her husband when she wants to.

Being a mother is normal, natural, easy, and glamorous. (Most mothers have blonde coifs by Mr. Kenneth, a gorgeous figure kept eternally that way, and a dazzling smile.)

Mothers are equally happy serving tomato soup, soothing hurts, bandaging cut knees, and turning a little snapper's mud-caked garments into a whiter-than-white wash.

A mother is a good amateur nutritionist, a superb disciplinarian (who need raise her voice only a notch to obtain obedience), an interior decorator, a gifted teacher, an expert in first aid, a *cordon bleu* chef, and a wonderful wife with a wonderful marriage. And she loves every minute of it.

So much for legend.

But the legend of American motherhood cannot be swept away by mocking it, however absurd it is. The legend clings and affects all our lives and thinking because it has been carefully fed and nourished for years by the mass media. Films, magazines, the women's pages of newspapers, and especially television have created a pervasive myth that victimizes every mother.

Consider the way mothers have been shown on a generation of soap operas. There's Nancy on "The Edge of Night," for instance. Nancy, who has a twenty-year-old stepdaughter, doesn't look a day over thirty. She is totally fulfilled by her role as wife and mother. Even early in the morning, the children are no bother. Fully and fashionably dressed and immaculately groomed, she sees her family off for the day. Good girl.

On the everlasting "As the World Turns," Lisa is another kind of person, a sort of super-villainess of the soaps. Yet she is saved from damnation by being a good mother. For all her problem over the years—an ongoing ordeal for which one can only admire the ingenuity of the scriptwriters—there was never a hint of maternal distress until after Lisa's oldest son grows up and is clued in on his Mom's transgressions with (would you believe?) men.

And that's the serious side of motherhood as shown on television. By night, the programming is a little different—it's eternally cheerful.

The classic nighttime TV mother, recently dispensing joy by day in coast-to-coast reruns, is Donna Reed of the show of the same name. She is young-looking and lovely, handles her children with a smile and a nod, and never raises her voice or hand to maintain fun-filled family harmony. Cool as twelve cucumbers.

Joan Nash, the mother of four rambunctious boys on

19

"Please Don't Eat the Daisies," goes Donna one trick better. Beautiful and totally happy, Joan is also talented: She writes. But her problems with her adorable kids are so trivial and so easily solved that there's time left over to put a little extra money in the family coffers by writing about their antics.

By the time you get to Mrs. Brady of "The Brady Bunch," you start to sense something else about TV mommies: They're rich. Or at least very, very comfortable. Mom Brady runs an enormous contemporary home (not to be confused with the enormous, tastefully decorated *old* home that Joan runs on "Please Don't Eat the Daisies"), is aided by a housekeeper who runs a close second to Mary Poppins, and always stays cool, collected, and ravishing while coping with her six well-behaved kids.

Things are much the same for Samantha on "Bewitched." *Her* problem is to forget she's a witch and just be a regular, beautiful, exquisitely groomed mommy in a regular, large, elegantly decorated house. But she never resorts to witchcraft when it comes to rearing the kids; for her—as it is presumably for all mommies—motherhood is a snap.

TV situation-comedy mothers (the situation-tragedy type are in short supply) are also ageless. On "My Three Sons," Katy and Bob had their absolutely delightful triplets while they were still going to college. But the demands of caring for their little ones have only added to their happiness over the years and don't seem to have made a dent in their freedom. They still go whipping off on vacations like carefree newlyweds. Perhaps Katy and Bob swig a lot of Geritol in the broom closet when no one's looking, but there's no evidence on camera.

You don't even have to be a woman to be a good mother on television. On "The Courtship of Eddie's Father," Dad is a widower (single parents on prime-time shows are almost never divorced) who not only puts average fathers to shame but makes most mothers look like slouches. He has all the paraphernalia: good looks, snappy wardrobe, a posh house, and a devoted housekeeper. Father and Eddie naturally spend a great deal of time together; they're so chummy, in fact, it's anybody's guess whether Dad ever works.

And the commercials on television go one step farther. Whether peddling baby products or homemaking aids, they always portray happy, immaculate, good-humored families, who are climbing into shiny new station wagons, eating cereal (which never winds up on the floor) in mushy or crunchy togetherness, brushing their teeth with abandon in a spontaneous quest for cavity-less good health, marveling over the whitening, qualities of one-syllable detergents, or ecstatically romping through fields of clover while an orchestra hidden in the highgrass accompanies then with a tender tune. Commercials for the likes of Pampers, Mennen baby products, Johnson & Johnson powder, Gerber's baby food, Playtex and even Jif peanut butter make motherhood seem the ultimate act of creativity and gracious living.

One recent commercial for Playtex nursers opened with a shot of an ordinary-looking woman feeding an ordinary-looking (and realistically cranky) baby with an ordinary-looking baby bottle. After a few beguiling words from the sponsor, presto!—the ordinary-looking mother and child (and bottle, of course) were replaced by a beautiful young mother and a beautiful bouncy baby, both serene with the Playtex nurser. Its nursing qualities aside, the bottle took ten years off the mother's age and gave her a new hairdo to boot.

To judge by TV commercials, the most serious decision a mother has to make is which brand of peanut butter to feed her family or which cleanser to make her kitchen sink sparkle. It would all be laughable if it were not so insidious. For not only is motherhood presented as easy, fun, and vastly fulfilling on TV, but it also is implicit that if life as a mother doesn't work for you the way it does on television, it could easily become so if you'd only buy a bushel or two of the sponsors' products.

It is no secret, even to the densest of us, that products can only be sold if a market is created for them. And by reinforcing the myth of perfect motherhood in commercials and on the shows themselves, American business is

21

creating a market for its products. Motherhood itself is sold as hard as any of the individual products—on the theory, presumably, that if you buy the myth, the products that make it all come true will be the next purchase.

And since television networks and magazines prosper on advertising, the networks and magazines (and the press in general) are likely to oblige by further feeding the motherhood myth. For a baby-food manufacturer is hardly likely to advertise in a magazine that extols the virtues of remaining childless. Whether advertisers actually control the content of the media may be debatable. What is beyond debate is that the cumulative message of the media is that motherhood is beautiful and a woman without children is an unhappy woman indeed.

As a mother who has experienced the realities of parenthood and has come to take it all quite seriously. I am insulted by the unrealistic and utterly frivolous way in which the mass media present motherhood. The mindless, plastic standards set up on the big and little screens and on the slick, colorful pages of nearly every popular magazine speak neither to the dignity nor to the travail of motherhood.

In the process of demeaning and trivializing women who have chosen (or had thrust upon them) motherhood as their life role, the importance of realistic and meaningful child guidance is ignored: housekeeping is presented not as a task to be done as speedily and efficiently as possible but as the glory of motherhood. Paradoxically, this false portrayal compounds the problems of parenthood because we come to feel, often without even noticing it, that unless we live up to the media-imposed standards of grace, we are failures as mothers.

Yet how can any of us help but fail in real life when measured against such a giddy standard? As I perform my daily janitorial services while coping with two active youngsters and trying to keep the spark in my marriage, I am confused and distressed by the images that the media constantly flaunt at me. For American industry's dandy products do not turn motherhood into bliss as the commercials suggest, any more than love alone does, as the whipped-cream programs suggest.

Love does not conquer all—neither romantically nor in dealing with children. Loving does not automatically equip a human being for the responsibility of caring for a young life (or lives), any more than it removes a parent's aversion to serving time on, say, a PTA committee. Neither love nor sudsier suds can make you like the responsibility, drudgery, or boredom that all mothers know deep down go with caring for their children.

Many women come to motherhood completely unaware of its drawbacks. And when they discover them, they often feel they are lacking as mothers if they somehow do not relish all the negatives, since a cardinal part of the motherhood myth is that *liking* being a mother is a must if you are to *be* a good mother.

I suppose there are actually a few mothers around who appear to have satisfied all the media and cultural standards of the perfect mother. They pull it all off. And their kids have no problems.

One such case dates back to my childhood, and I'll never forget her. I was about ten years old when her daughter Erika came to our school. None of us had ever seen a wardrobe quite like Erika's. Her mother designed and made most of her gorgeous clothes. Her hair shimmered with golden curls (made perfect by appointments at the beauty parlor), and she wore heirloom jewelry and had a wristwatch. On top of which she was actually nice.

Erika's mother walked her down the street looking like Grace Kelly. She wore prescription sunglasses and had on a camel's hair polo coat and led the family's pedigreed dog on a long leash. And their house was exquisite ("Mother does all the decorating and made some of the furniture—the rest are genuine antiques.")

Naturally, Erika made straight A's in school. She had riding lessons, piano lessons, drawing lessons, swimming lessons, and voice lessons. She went to college and became the Sweetheart of Sigma Chi, belonged to the best sorority, graduated with honors, married the captain of the football team—I won't even mention the wedding, teas, and all the trimmings—and took her Master's at Stanford.

It was years later, and well after I had had children, that I discovered that things had not been exactly as they seemed with Erika and her mother. Erika and I accidentally bumped into each other and reminisced. Things came out. Like the shoplifting bouts that went on during most of her childhood. Like how she had tried to commit suicide at sixteen. Like the nights she sneaked out after her parents were asleep, taking the family car (without having a driver's license) to meet one of many boys. She explained how, long years before, she had changed a teacher's grade book to maintain her straight A average— because if she didn't get all A's, her parents would have beaten the hell out of her. We then talked about her disastrous marriage, her divorce, her psychiatrist, and her generally unhappy life.

Some parents make it look so easy that their children never recover.

There may or may not be such a thing as a perfect mother. But it is clear there are women at the other end of the scale who don't do well at all as mothers because they can't—and no one expects them to. These "remarkable" women (as in: "What a remarkable woman—how she manages with all those kids, I'll never know!") keep producing child after child, often with the blessings of family, friends, and society. And it doesn't matter whether such a woman is equipped emotionally, intellectually, or physically to do a decent job of raising her children. If she makes a mess of it, she is likely to be forgiven.

Jane, one of the mothers I interviewed at length, has five girls. She is truly a remarkable woman—she wants more children. She hates housework, admits the kids drive her up the wall, and is in chronic poor health. But she remains committed to continued reproducing.

I wonder deeply about such mothers who continue to have children long after they have come to grips with the realities of parenthood. I can understand the handful of gifted mothers who are equipped to rear children with all the resources—physical, intellectual, emotional, and financial. And I can understand the pressures on Catholic women who really feel they have no choice if they are to adhere to their faith. But what of the others? Sheer masochism doesn't seem to cover it. Could it be that even in the face of reality, the motherhood myths are so strong that they persuade women to try again and again to have a child that will finally make the myth come true?

Most of the women I spoke with while preparing this book were neither perfect mothers nor "remarkable" women. They were what I think of as typical middle-class women with typical problems and rewards during the course of parenthood. Let's consider three of them.

Lou Anne is a warm, vivacious, and loving woman whose affection for her kids is as persuasive as the most convincing brand on any television show. When she was pregnant with the last of her four children, her husband suggested that an abortion might be in order. Lou Anne wouldn't discuss it—the idea was too repugnant for her even to consider it. But seven years later, she willingly discusses it. She says with conviction that if she had it to do all over again, not only would she have had the abortion, but she would have had no children at all. For Lou Anne, being a mother has meant fifteen years of fear, guilt, feelings of inadequacy, and the struggle to pursue her own interests against overwhelming odds. She says:

I love the children—I'd die if anything happened to any one of them, but I detest being a mother.

She had never given much thought to what it would mean to be a mother; it just seemed the natural thing following marriage. By the time she confronted the problems raised by her youngsters in high school, she felt as if the walls were closing in on her.

Oh, I know that everyone thinks I have it made, and many of our friends think of me as the epitome of a happy, fulfilled mother. I'm sure many of them would be surprised to learn that they're only seeing the outer wrapper. Underneath I'm constantly surprised and frus-

25

trated by all that's involved in doing a half-decent job with the kids. It's such damned hard work, and it's not work that I enjoy. When the kids were younger, I never really felt good—I was almost always slightly ill. The struggle to remain a self has been an arduous one. But what's worse is that, having made it through the drudgery and chaos of handling small children, I'm now moving into the gut-tearing worry of guiding them through their teens.

Dianne is the twenty-six-year-old mother of two adorable children and could easily compete with the pretty models on TV commercials. This is what she says about motherhood:

Nobody ever told me there were rotten sides to it. You just don't happen to think about it. I don't mind changing diapers—changing diapers is no big deal to me —that's minimal. I didn't think about all the other stuff. I didn't think about how hard it would be—how my life would be changed. I didn't know how I would completely lose my freedom—not just the freedom to come and go as I pleased but the freedom to put my own needs above those of my children without wondering if it's affecting them adversely.

My first view of motherhood was that if you do everything right, take care of the kid, change his diapers, and all that—you can make it. Now that I have kids, I know better.

When I asked Dianne if she felt she were equipped for motherhood, she said:

No. Everyone thinks I'm a great mother. Most of the time, I'm even-tempered, I'm nice to the kids, and I really like them. . . . But I don't really want them—I'd be happier without them, but I probably could never have gotten out of the cultural thing of having them. I'm sure that no one would ever believe that if I didn't have children, it would be because I chose not to have any. But I find such joy in them, and I love them so— it's all very confusing.

26

Kelly is the mother of two planned children. She gets right to the point:

The kids are great. The only problem we have is that the kids I love got stuck with a lousy mother. I didn't know in advance that I'm no good at this.

Lou Anne, Dianne, and Kelly are only three of the many women I spoke with who feel they are less than sterling mothers. Yet on the face of it, they are probably three of the most dedicated and proficient. They love their children, and the kids look just fine. They don't go off to work and leave their youngsters with babysitters—a reliable way to dredge up a lot of guilt. Why, then, don't they think they are good mothers? Almost certainly, the problem is traceable to the image of motherhood these women carry around in their heads—that great myth that says a mother is a person who loves being a mother, who finds being a mother a snap, who is completely fulfilled by the role, whose children are happy all the time, and whose severest negative feeling toward her kids is one of mild annoyance.

Other mothers I spoke with were more severely afflicted by the myths and realities of motherhood—and the gap between the two. Lynn, for example, is able to function apparently as well as any TV mother, thanks largely to her psychiatrist and her tranquilizers. But before she sought help, this is how she felt:

I thought I knew what depression was—until I really experienced it. God, I tried hard to fight it, but I didn't seem to have the strength. I just simply didn't care any more. Nothing was very important to me, even the kids, who have always been so dear to me. I just got to feeling that the only reason for me to exist is that the kids needed someone to take care of them. I guess the reason it got to me is that while I had all the responsibility for the kids, the rewards were slim and sandwiched in between what seemed an endless number of crises, enormous confusion, and the increasing feeling that I was a failure as a mother. It didn't help that my husband didn't understand.

It's odd. When I was growing up, my parents always told me that I was important just because I was me. And now I get the feeling that I'm important only because I'm a mother and the children need me.

Esther is a real-life mother who has never managed to reconcile motherhood with a career because she has never been able to stay at anything long enough for things to work out. She feels she's forever batting zero where her personal interests are concerned. Now and then she manages some volunteer work in a social welfare organization, and she's been going to school for *years*—years, because she keeps having to drop out to meet what she feels are the legitimate demands of her family. She seems to be truly fulfilled by her children, but she dwells on the endless struggle to find a little piece of life that is her very own.

Joy is a mother who, unlike Esther, really made it through school. Once her kids were at school all day, she picked up her own education again. She timed everything to coincide with the children's hours of need, but the responsibilities that go with a family while she was trying to study on her own nearly drove her mad. She finally got her degree the same week her son got his high school diploma. The price came high.

Lillie is a mother and a pianist. She has a little boy whom she describes as "absolutely terrific," but she told me that if she had known ten years ago what she knows now, she would have followed up her contraceptive failure with an abortion.

Sure, I resent him. The responsibility is overwhelming. I have a career that means a great deal to me, and I will not abandon it. But it is incredibly difficult to be both a good musician and the kind of mother I think I should be. My work involves travel and staying away

28

from home for days at a time. I feel guilty about leaving my child. A mother always does, I guess.

Gloria is a happy mother. She says as much. She has five boys who seem to keep the family in perpetual financial distress. She often laments that they can't afford decent clothes for all the kids. Yet several nights a week, you can find Gloria and her husband elbow-bending at a popular bar in town and having a high old time of it. Invariably when she's high, Gloria gets sentimental about the children and talks glowingly of the joys of motherhood, starting with the first labor pain. (Actually, Gloria doesn't spend all her recreational time in bars. During the day, she generally entertains at home, serving generous drinks, whether or not she has any guests.) For some women, it works best to keep the motherhood-reality gap open: It may be the only way they can make it.

Betty is a mother without a husband. After getting over the shock of the divorce and the dramatic change in her style and standard of living, she misses adult companionship the way any thirty-five-year-old would. During the week she works, and evenings and weekends she copes with the kids, so that when some man does ask her out, she wants to jump at the chance. Maternal guilt, though, keeps getting in the way, because:

. . . the kids really have only me, and I'm gone all day long. I just feel that however much I want to get out of the house or would like to go out with a man, it's really unfair to shunt the children off with a babysitter. And when I do, I can hardly enjoy myself because I feel so terribly guilty.

Sharon is not a typical mother nor a typical divorcée. But her story is important because it did happen to her and can to others.

Sharon was eighteen when she got married. Her husband was a graduate student at New York University, and she was entering her freshman year. She's bright,

29

tough, and intuitive, and when she married young, she looked ahead and saw the future blueprinted. They would be a happy married couple, getting all their respective degrees, finding good jobs, and raising great kids—all just like the great-looking, two-child family in all the Chevrolet commercials.

It didn't work. One year after marriage, Sharon gave birth to a daughter; fourteen months after that, a son. A year after that, she and her husband separated. He had no money to give her, and her middle-class suburban parents refused to give her any help, saying that she had made her bed and now she could lie in it.

She applied for a job at a public library on the strength of one year of library training at N.Y.U., but she was told, "We don't generally hire women with young children." It was no easier finding work elsewhere. She moved to a tiny apartment on the Lower East Side and continued to seek work. By the time she applied for welfare assistance, she was desperate. But because she and her husband were still legally married, she was turned down.

Truly desperate now, she took a clerical position paying $57 a week. She had to place the children in a neighborhood day-care center and then hire someone to pick them up at the end of the day because she couldn't get out of work to do it herself by the time the center closed. When she got home, she made dinner, fed the children, left them alone while she ran down to the laundromat, came back and bathed them, bedded them down—and then prepared for the next dismal day.

Under such circumstances, $57 doesn't go very far, especially in New York. A resourceful woman, Sharon learned how to steal food while doing the marketing—especially meat, since she couldn't afford to give them as much as she felt they needed. One day, after months of this grinding routine, she took a good look at her situation and realized that she and her children were trapped in this way of life. The only solution for them and for herself was painful in the extreme:

I knew I was giving them up for several weeks before the appointed time. I could hardly look at them without crying. I'd see their little open faces looking at me—they knew something was going on—and I'd go into the bathroom and cry. Finally I called the agency and told them that I couldn't take it any longer, that I had to do it now.

I had picked one of the best agencies in New York, and I was told that if I brought them up the next day, the children would be temporarily placed in a foster home until they could be placed permanently.

The next day I dressed them for the last time and took them to the agency. They were so precious—two little peas in a pod. Anyway, I went up to the seventh floor of the agency—it was beautifully appointed with nice furniture, thick carpets, and wall hangings. Someone came out into the waiting room and, after a brief exchange, she led them away. The door simply closed and I was alone. It was a few minutes later when I realized I hadn't seen those things on my last visit to the agency.

I asked her, "What things?"

The bars on the windows. I only noticed them when I wanted to jump. And I knew why they were there—and how many before me had wanted to just to make it stop hurting.

The physical and mental well-being of American mothers and the stability of the American family require that we face up to the gap between the myth and the realities of motherhood. Dr. Benjamin Spock, probably the nation's most highly regarded authority on child care, even after all these years, notes that the difficulty begins with the fact that ours is a highly child-centered culture. When our media-fed cultural attitudes, telling us that parenthood is normal, natural, fun, and easy, collide with a child-centered society that makes parenthood a very hard job indeed, a kind of schizophrenia results and leads to the kinds of confusion and frustration reflected in the words of the mothers cited above.

For all of modern life's conveniences, being a parent is perhaps more difficult today than ever before. And we'd better begin facing it. At every age level and in almost all places, there are new and more dangers for children. While we no longer have to fear their being scalped by marauding Indians as our forebears did, the threats today are far from trivial. Rapid population growth has turned quiet suburban streets into potential traffic hazards. Air pollution has produced allergies that previously would have remained latent. Pesticides and poisons not only damage the land but the youngsters as well. And anyone reading the newspapers for a single day knows that the problems of adolescence are more severe than ever—the automobile, drugs, sexual promiscuity, thievery for thrills.

All these cultural factors add to the increasing demands on parents. We send our kids to school to learn to read and write, and we wind up having to teach them ourselves because the curriculum has been expanded without a corresponding increase in class time or teacher supervision. And social pressures have escalated unmercifully. The child who doesn't belong to some scouting group or go to dancing class or to museums with his parents can be truly a deprived child, at least on a comparative basis. If parents don't "interact" with the schools, they are likely to be thought uninterested in their children. Volunteering for car pools or to bake a cake or to chaperone a field trip becomes almost obligatory.

Beyond that, the abundance of child-guidance experts and theories is a double-edged sword. As much as guidance can help, it also confuses and hinders. Much of the counsel we are offered today conflicts not only with traditional methods and thinking but also with other current views on the same subjects. One pediatrician, for example, may advise that children need plenty of rest and that however reluctant they may be to go to bed, they should be firmly bedded down at an early hour. Shortly after following this advice, I came across an article in *McCall's* by a pair of experts with seemingly impressive credentials who asserted that parents put their children to bed too early, often because they just want to get them out of the way. The experts argue that this is bad for the kids, who understand and feel rejected. An argument can be made that maybe we were better off in the bygone days when we merely trusted our instincts and never cracked a book or listened to a lecture. That day, we might have been wrong, but as least we were consistently so.

The plain truth is that being a mother is the most important, difficult, and demanding of careers. At stake is the very life of another human being—and almost total responsibility for that life during its formative years. E. James Lieberman, a psychiatrist formerly with the National Institute of Mental Health writes:

> Child-rearing is the most difficult task that most ordinary mortals will ever undertake. It is the first priority of this and every nation, costly to do well and costlier to neglect. We are not doing a good enough job. We can do better, but the challenge is sobering.[1]

This succinct statement by Dr. Lieberman and this from the federally financed *Report of the Commission on Population Growth and the American Future* adds fuel to the need to demythicize parenthood:

> . . . We tend to overlook the fact that we are not all equally suited for parenthood any more than we are for teaching school or playing various sports. Matters of temperament, age, health, and competing interests, to mention just a few, are considerations in determining whether or not to have children.[2]

A sober outlook on the world would suggest to us that there is a balance between the good and the bad in life— in a job, in a marriage, in a parent-child relationship. Many women come to feel, as I do, that the scales of motherhood do not really balance out for them, that the

33

rewards of motherhood—and they are indeed there, and nothing here is meant to suggest otherwise—are not great enough to offset the difficulties and plain unpleasantness of so much of the job. This is not to say that many mothers who find the job of mothering unrewarding feel that they have been handed a distinctly rotten bill of goods. Instead of questioning the image of idealized motherhood, once they have a truer sense of the real burdens involved, they begin to question themselves. The fault lies in themselves, many mothers feel, and nowhere else.

For other mothers, the rewards are enough. They derive so much joy from so many things about their small babies that they are shocked when other mothers question the giving-and-getting ratio. For these joyous mothers, it is very hard to understand how any mother can feel, as a friend of mine did, that "One lousy little smile from a three-month-old isn't worth the loss of freedom for those three months or the changing of a hundred dirty diapers."

Other mothers don't feel the imbalance until later—until, say, their youngsters are toddlers or perhaps even of school age and more demanding. It's then, in these cases, when the question of getting as good as you give is presented in bolder relief. And, when resenting the things about parenthood that one might be expected to resent is heightened by not enjoying enough the things that one might be expected to enjoy, the whole process can turn into a nightmare.

And yet most women still look inside themselves for the answer, still make the assumption that the source of the imbalance must lie within them. Perhaps, in some cases, it does—perhaps a woman who takes little joy in being a mother is lacking as a woman. But there are so many of us who feel this imbalance that perhaps we can begin to understand that, though we may be lacking, we are not unusual. And if we are not unusual, then we are not unnatural.

Motherhood, then, is both a career and an affliction. It has caused many women to seek nothing beyond, caused many others to stifle their creative spirits and their dreams for a career of a different order, and caused still others to wear themselves out trying to do justice to two careers.

In place of the legend and the myths at the outset of this chapter, defining what a mother is, perhaps a different roster of values—and higher fidelity to the truth—can be offered at the close.

A mother is being away from home and missing your children terribly, only to come back and be greeted by, "What did you bring me?" And finding what you brought (and spent a couple of hours shopping for, nearly missing the plane) broken into a dozen pieces two days later.

A mother is feeling that the children should have a pet—a nice little dog, say—because all children should grow up with a pet. And then taking the dog to the vet, feeding it, cleaning up after it, nearly breaking a leg tripping over it, keeping it from getting hit by a car, and then looking at the critter one day and thinking, "My God, that thing is just as much trouble as another child would be."

A mother is having someone small hovering about you constantly—stepping on your feet, absently fooling around with something useful (or anything at all) and breaking it, doing his or her little project one foot away from wherever it is you are doing whatever you are doing, or running in every two minutes and cutting into your thoughts with, "Lookit what I made, Mom," or "Why is the sky blue, Mom?" or "I didn't mean to break the lamp, Mom," or "Mom! There's a big spider in the living room!" And all the while not losing your patience. Then there's that sinking feeling after the final interruption—the one that goes, "Mom, I love you so much"—gets to you. To lose your patience just at the moment your child is expressing affection is pain that only a mother can know.

A mother is knowing the dark fear of having a sick or hurt child, feeling your stomach and knees cave in at the sight of a bloody head—and the guilt that whatever is wrong might have been prevented if you were better at your job.

A mother is feeling hostility toward the man you love

when he speaks sharply to your child and hurts the child's feelings—and an hour later resenting the same child for having triggered another nasty little argument between two grownups who otherwise wouldn't be arguing.

A mother is knowing what it's like to have every one of your senses bombarded with questions, noise, and misbehavior until, at the peak of the bombardment, you wonder if your mind has deteriorated to such an extent that it will never again be able to concentrate even on a simple thought. It is feeling that where thoughts once lingered, there is now a total void.

A mother is accepting that you must do many things that you are entirely uninterested in doing simply because you are a mother. It is knowing not to make comparisons between your relationship with your husband and your relationship with your children. Even in non-egalitarian marriages, the relationship between husband and wife is a matter of give and take toward each other. The relationship between a mother and her children is that she gives and they take.

A mother is feeling the most profound love possible for another human being—or several of them. It is knowing that however much of a disaster you may be as a mother, however much terror you feel over coping with the responsibility each day, you couldn't bear to live without your children.

A mother is also me.

I have two lovely, healthy, intelligent, wanted children. I love them more than life. I try to take good care of them and struggle to guide them well. But if being a mother means liking the job, I am a failure at it.

The truth is that I don't like being a service machine, a janitor, a laundress, a nurse, a room mother or PTA stalwart or referee of children's sparring matches.

I'm a lousy disciplinarian. I'm nervous. And I detest camping, so my kids will never have the thrill of catching trout (or cold) in the Sierras—at least not with me along. I lose my cool when they're sick, injured, or have their feelings hurt by other people or even by me. I'm not really very well cut out for my role, and my kids deserve better than they got.

2

Pressure to bear

THE EIGHT YEARS BEFORE we had children were glorious.
We lived in a tiny, charming house, furnished with an
assortment of antiques and junk selected during many
happy hours of rummaging through shoppes and flea mar-
kets. The house sat in the middle of a huge lot, and by
our own labor we added a swimming pool and, around it
a terrace of three thousand bricks.

Our home was a paradise, a perpetual retreat.

During those eight years, I followed an enjoyable and
rewarding career. And our home life made the end of the
work day yet one more experience to anticipate with pleasure. Each night my husband and I would both race home
from work, have cocktails, watch the evening news, trade
gossip and the day's developments while I tried out some
new recipe. We had friends, we entertained often, and we
traveled when we felt like it. We would go to Mexico, to
far-off cities to visit friends, and sometimes, just for the
hell of it, we spent weekends in San Francisco, thirty-five
miles away.

We also enjoyed going to movies on the spur of the
moment, to the theater, meeting after work for dinner out
somewhere cozy or fancy, or just spending an hour brows-
ing in a book store.

Yet to our astonishment, we found that friends and acquaintances *pitied* us because we were childless.

If we heard it once, we heard it a thousand times:
"When are you going to start your family?" It was always

conveyed with an air of deep concern. "Anything wrong with you?" they would ask solicitously. That one was usually addressed to me since it's considered bad form to ask a man (although my husband got some of this from the boys in the locker room). "Have you had tests?" was common. "I can recommend a good gynecologist" was offered every other day, it seemed.

We got it even from my sister, who not too subtly suggested at one point that unless I experienced the miracle of having a child, I would never truly be a woman.

In retrospect, I want to express my sincere appreciation of all those who offered their concern to us. No doubt, they were worried that we might go on living a hedonistic, meaningless, if terribly comfortable life unless we became parents.

I know a few other pitied women who have elected to remain childless. And while they may evoke sympathy from others, from me they will have to settle for envy.

One couple we know decided, after five years of marriage and careful reflection, to remain childless. They have a beautiful home, enjoy careers that utilize their talents to the fullest, go camping and skiing as and when they like (rather than forcing themselves to as many parents do largely for the sake of their children), have traveled widely in Europe and the Orient—and are very much in love after ten years of marriage. Nothing in their natures suggests that they have neuroses that would lead to their childless state. They are warm and loving and appear genuinely to like children.

Every once in a while, this couple drops in on a moment's notice to visit old friends. Occasionally we are the old friends they come to see. They seem young and healthy and full of good cheer when they greet us. How sad I am for them, though. They will never know the enriching experience of having to plan such visits three weeks in advance. As another friend of ours, a father of four, puts it:

These poor creatures will never experience the challenge of vacationing with four kids, the joy of camping with

41

two other families with a total of ten children to keep them on their toes. Or the fun of planning an evening at the movies with the arrangements closely resembling in precision and detail the strategy of the D-Day landing at Normandy.

Then there is my friend and former co-worker, Carol, who is married and planning a law career. At the moment, she is convinced that she can be fulfilled without children. She's still young, and perhaps she'll change her mind; she certainly has been under enough pressure to conceive. Asked about it for the hundredth time recently, she answered, "I'm more of a world-saver than anything else, and it wouldn't be easy for me to save the world if I had children who needed my attention constantly."

The answer she got was: "You should have a child and hope that *he'll* save the world." Carry that kind of thinking to its logical extreme, and each generation would defer its ambitions to the next one—forever.

Bill and Martha are going through serious problems caused by pressure to start a family. The very fact that this is a source of controversy *now* should be a warning to them. He wants children, or has been convinced that he does; she doesn't, and has made her feelings crystal clear to everyone since before their marriage. Some of their acquaintances—all parents, of course—have judged her a vain, cold, and selfish woman. These so-called friends, with their clucking over the childless state of the couple, have added fuel to what should be a private controversy.

No one has yet suggested that Martha has confidence enough in her femininity, and is sufficiently happy with her husband and their life style, not to need *more* for fulfillment—a compliment to them both. Nor has anyone offered the advice that if Bill pushes her into having a child she doesn't want—forces her through pregnancy, childbirth, drudgery, worry, guilt, and abandonment of her career—he is gambling with their marriage. Besides, he knew in advance (as did everyone else) that Martha never wanted children. It's pretty late to change the ground rules now.

At a cocktail party recently, we ran into some old friends whom we hadn't seen for a long time and learned that their oldest son had been married for a while. When I made the standard comment that it was hard to believe since it seemed only yesterday that he was a gangly teenager with braces on his teeth, his mother lamented that children grow up all too quickly. She added she was hopeful her son and his wife wouldn't wait too long before presenting her with a grandchild. She went on to explain that her son's wife didn't want children, but they hoped to "bring her around." Apparently our friends thought it perfectly natural for this young woman to have children she didn't want just so she could please her in-laws.

That this attitude is common among potential grandparents is suggested by letters to two sisters who give advice in separate syndicated newspaper columns:

DEAR ABBY:

I have a twenty-seven-year-old daughter who is no raving beauty, but she is a lot better looking than most of the girls whose pictures you see in bridal veils in the Sunday papers. She is very intelligent and has lots of dates, and I know she has turned down several good marriage proposals.

When I ask her what she is waiting for, she says, "Don't rush me, Mom."

Is there any way I can get her to hurry up and think seriously of marrying and settling down? I am fifty years old and would like to see a few grandchildren before I leave this earth.

MOM

DEAR MOM:

Many moms who have rushed their daughters into marriage see more of their grandchildren than they expected to. (They're raising them because the marriage didn't work out.) If you're eager to see things hatch, settle down on a chicken farm.

To reinforce her very good advice, Abby might have referred "Mom" to this letter appearing in her sister's column:

DEAR ANN LANDERS:

Please tell newlyweds not to have children unless they really want them. My husband and I have been married sixteen years. We have three sons. We didn't want any of them. His parents kept bribing us and we were foolish enough to go for it.

Every argument we have is over the boys. Our marriage would be perfect if it weren't for these monsters. They have ruined our relationship.

If we weren't afraid of what people would say we'd put them all up for adoption. We've discussed it many times but we don't have the nerve . . . I hope you print [this letter] for the benefit of young people who are very much in love—as we were, once. I'd give anything to turn back the clock.

THRICE ERRED

Nor does social coercion end after you've had one or two children. We know several couples who have an "only child," and they are constantly harassed. They expect it to continue right up to menopause. "When are you going to have another baby?" becomes all too familiar and tedious. In a letter a friend of mine writes: "We have one baby, and would like to keep the number of children to one. Already (our baby is one month old) we are getting pressure about having a second one."

Another woman put it this way:

I've often thought how screwed up our ideal marriage became after our child arrived, but that's not the kind of thing you're supposed to admit, even to yourself, let alone anyone else. I was never an emotional pillar of strength, but I've quickly exhausted my stability in these last couple of years.

I fear that my wonderful daughter deserved a better

mother. I don't deny my deep love for her, but I have denied my deep resentment and unhappiness with motherhood. The result has been frequent bouts of rage and loss of control—outbursts that have frightened me into seeking psychiatric help. Yet most of the advice I get from my bedraggled domesticated friends has been: "Get pregnant again—you'll be so busy with two children you won't have time for those unnatural feelings of yours."

Even if this young woman does have a second child—a prospect she says fills her with real terror—chances are the pressure still wouldn't end. After our second child was born, we were constantly asked when we were going to have a third. Recently, a neighbor, sighting a group of children playing nearby, asked me which ones were mine. When I pointed out our pair, her face registered a combination of pity and disdain as she asked: "Is that *all?*"

The pressure is clearly greater when a couple is divided on the subject. A frantic young father of three told me:

Caring for our three daughters is all I can manage, both financially and emotionally. But my wife won't let up. She thinks she wants six kids, and I know I'd go beserk with that kind of responsibility. At times I almost think she'd *like* to see me fall apart at the seams. She wants to get pregnant again so much that I fear she lies to me about using contraceptives. You can imagine what that's doing to our sex life. It's becoming nonexistent simply because my terror over having more kids causes periodic impotence.

When I asked why his wife wanted so many children, he said, "I think she wants to keep up with her mother, who keeps needling her for not following her example—it's a status thing, I guess."

Why should the decisions by these couples regarding their own families—an area of presumably great privacy—be open to question by relatives, friends, or neighbors? People who *have* children are not challenged daily on

45

their choice or chided for their contraceptive failures. Why should it be socially acceptable among many people to ask a childless couple why they don't have any children—but unacceptable to ask prolific breeders why they have so *many* children? We don't tell other people what kind of jobs they should hold or work they should do, whom they should marry or where they should take their vacations. And it is generally considered rude to inquire into the financial affairs of other people. Yet their breeding habits, if they're childless (or even if they're not), are somehow considered fair game.

Even utterly miserable couples with children have scant hesitation about urging everyone else to follow their example. Perhaps it's simply a matter of misery loving company. Or maybe they're the prototypes of what H. L. Mencken called "wowsers"—people "tormented by the thought that someone, somewhere, might be having a good time." Consider for a moment that most potent of rebukes that a parent can dish out to a child: "Just wait till *you* have children of your own."

As a Catholic, once devout, I am acutely aware of a major source of pressure to procreate affecting about 25 percent of the American people. Not content with spreading the word about how nice and fulfilling it is to have babies, the Catholic Church is capable of exerting powerful force to see that it happens that way.

To be faithful to the teaching of the Church (*His* teachings, it is implicitly or explicitly noted), devout Catholics have but three choices: have babies as the heavens decree; practice the rhythm method of birth control; or abstain. The fourth choice, of course, is to break with the Church and use conventional methods of birth control —a course that growing numbers of Catholics are taking. But many others, unwilling to defy the Church, find themselves miserably trapped by their adherence to dogma. Consider these remarks to me by Lydia, a sixty-year-old mother of nine.

Looking back to my time, the pressure young folks got to have kids was unbearable, at least in the Midwest where my husband, Herb, and I were living at the time. Besides being surrounded by Catholic relatives who would have been shocked if I didn't get pregnant at least every two years, there was the parish priest. Herb is a much more devout Catholic than I am, so if I had suggested contraception or spacing, he would have been deeply hurt. I love him to this day, and I couldn't disappoint him. The only birth control that ever worked for us was abstinence. For two people terribly in love, it was hell. After about seven or eight months of not touching each other, we'd both lose our heads and I'd always wind up pregnant.

So the great pressure to have children came from the love of my life. He couldn't help it, the poor dear—he thought he was abiding by the Lord's teachings. Today, in this age of enlightenment, the Church's rules seem insipid—*now* we wouldn't believe such nonsense.

With a bitter laugh, Lydia added that when she wasn't pregnant as a younger woman, her husband and she avoided physical contact as much as possible—"to keep me that way. But people still talked, little remarks that implied all we did was screw. It was damned if you did and damned if you didn't."

More and more, though, Catholics are deciding that they cannot reconcile the Church's present position on birth control with either Scripture or the problems of parenthood. They are reading books and other publications that hold that not only is the Church's policy a man-made rule but that the Church has not always practiced what it preaches—or always preached the same thing. Growing numbers of priests and laymen are adopting more rational attitudes toward family planning. Unfortunately, many Catholics become "enlightened" only after the facts have been painfully demonstrated by their many offspring.

Not unlike Lydia, Donna decided that the Church's attitude on birth control was both silly and cruel—but by then she had six children.

After Amy was born, I wouldn't let my husband get

near me for six months. It was agony for us both, but I was terrified at the thought of another pregnancy. I did some heavy thinking, and was lucky to have a Catholic friend to talk to. She had practiced birth control most of her married life and persuaded me that the Church's position wasn't logical—probably because I wanted to be persuaded. I still get angry that the Church nearly destroyed my relationship with my husband. What right do a bunch of old celibates have to tell young healthy lovers that they can't have sex without babies? Sex isn't dirty. It's beautiful. And between a man and woman who really dig each other, it's as close to Heaven as I care to be for now.

This kind of healthy rebellion gains strength from the growing realization that the Church's position on birth control is curiously flexible. If a woman's menstrual cycle is out of whack, she can take oral contraceptives to straighten herself out—in which case birth control becomes just a convenient fringe benefit. But who determines how severely or how slightly a woman's menstrual cycle is out of schedule and requires straightening? If your cycle is one day out of line, why shouldn't you do something about it—and derive the fringe benefits in the bargain? Temporary sterility is also sometimes correctable by the sanctioned taking of oral contraceptives for a few months and then stopping.

I find this all quite interesting. You can take oral contraceptives to help you have babies, but you can't take them to keep from having babies.

The pressure to reproduce directed at young adults is heightened still further by that greatest of the American persuaders—the mass media. The message comes over loud and clear: A woman isn't a woman until she's a mother.

Daytime television is especially insistent on reinforcing the position that a woman is not fulfilled unless she has offspring. Commercials, touched upon in the previous chapter, might be expected to push for babies since so

48

many of the sponsors are in the baby business. The daytime soaps are almost slavish in picking up the cue. The result is some of the most bizarre and involved plotting ever devised by man.

On "Love Is a Many Splendored Thing," one of the most blatant cases involved the story of a young woman whose miscarriage—and miscarriages are of course treated as full-scale disasters on most shows—left her sterile, thereby nearly ruining her life since she could not become fulfilled as a woman. Her sister, meanwhile, was in a plane crash and suffered brain damage that produced blindness. Then, as they usually do on such shows, things got worse: The woman's case was diagnosed as terminal. Her fiancé nevertheless insisted that they marry—and after her selfless protests that she would be a burden, she agreed. And in a flash became pregnant.

Fearing that the strain would foreshorten her already waning life, her husband urged an abortion. She would have none of it: She meant to leave him a son, at whatever cost. After six months of pregnancy, it was apparent her end was near. A delivery by Caesarean section was the only solution, and a race ensued between the stork and the grim reaper. The stork won, happily, and we all waited for the brave young woman to breathe her noble last. But no! The birth somehow relieved the pressure on her brain (I'm not entirely clear how that works, unless perhaps her organs were more mobile than most), and her life was spared. As an extra added miracle, the new Mom regained her sight. Ain't babies grand?

Some TV heroines will do anything to have a baby (as should all of us, the implicit message reads). Take Audrey, on "General Hospital." Married to the chief of staff at the hospital, whom she called "Darling" all the time—I thought that was his name—she had a blissful marriage. The only fly in the ointment was that after two years of wedlock, she had not conceived and was mighty blue. Tests confirmed her suspicion that the fault wasn't hers, and so, thinking to protect her marriage and preserve her husband's *macho* image of himself, she forged his signa-

49

ture on documents and flew off to another part of the country to be artificially inseminated.

Eight months pregnant, Audrey was injured in a car crash, lost her baby, and was rendered sterile. Naturally, she and her husband were divorced. Uncertain what the moral was—it seemed to be either 1. a baby is worth deceiving your husband for, or 2. childless wives are worthless wives and should be disposed of after three years—I lost track of the program for many months. When I tuned back in recently, all manner of things had gone on. First off, Audrey was remarrying her doctor husband, whose name now seems to be Steve. But it was no easy trick to arrange.

An enterprising girl, Audrey has kidnapped a baby, and she has been keeping the tot stashed in the apartment of a babysitter who doesn't quite dig what's going on. Or so I thought. Actually, it turns out the baby is really Audrey's because after divorcing Steve, she married Tom, but that didn't work out so hot either, so they were calling it quits when Audrey discovered that she was expecting. Happy day! She leaves town and Tom, and heads to another part of the country—a free spirit, that Audrey—and gives birth in a hospital she has entered under her maiden name. Returning to her home town, where Steve still is, Audrey places the baby with a sort of full-time babysitter but doesn't tell her who the mother is—clearly this is one of the less alert babysitters in America. Audrey then picks up with Steve, readies to re-tie the knot, and convinces him that they should adopt an orphan. Got it?

The matter of how Audrey's severed Fallopian tubes were put back together so she could have her baby bothers me a bit. Perhaps it was will power. More likely, the show's writers found a way one day when I wasn't watching. It was imperative that Audrey's image as "a whole woman" be restored—viewers may have found her sterility intolerable, and maybe the show's ratings were dropping accordingly—and where there's a will, we all know, there's a way.

In general, any woman on daytime serials who prefers

50

a career to children is viewed as misguided if not actively wicked. And any woman who doesn't want to have children is depicted as vain, selfish, cold, more than likely disturbed emotionally, and positively headed for unhappiness and lovelessness.

Susan on "As the World Turns" preferred a career in medicine to motherhood, and her folly produced a great deal of disapproval and the warning that she was jeopardizing her marriage to Dan. And sure enough, Dan starts fooling around with another woman. Before long, he is getting ready to leave Susan to her medicine and set up a new nest. Susan gets the picture and, without excessive remorse, seduces her own husband in an effort to become pregnant. Success is hers, and Dan stays home. Susan, too.

On one soap (I forget which—they all tend to blend into one another after a while), a young woman is impregnated as a result of rape. Her first inclination is of course to get an abortion, but her compassionate aunt soon talks her out of it. Once the child arrives and the joy of childbirth experienced, the circumstances of the conception are forgotten and the new mother is at peace.

Week after week, month after month, year after year, and paid for in part by the captains of the baby products business, these shows deliver one unmistakable message. And to drive the point home harder, the babies and children on the shows are all quite spotless, wear picture-book clothes, never make a mess, and seldom if ever cry. To judge by the soaps, you'd think that babies never require a change of diapers.

Evening programming reinforces the daytime fare and is probably even more influential with the pre-motherhood sector of the population. A woman on evening TV is allowed to be single so long as it is quite clear that one day she'll put her career aside and settle down to raise a husky, wholesome family. And there is no such thing as a childless couple on any show—except of course Oscar and Felix on "The Odd Couple." And no one really expects them to cement their relationship with a baby. (Besides which, they aren't even married.)

But no pressure can be compared to the greatest pressure of all toward parenthood—the pressure from within. The bland and unthinking assumption of most women that they must become mothers has been conditioned no doubt by thousands of years of civilization that have made the prospect of a woman who chooses to remain motherless a frightening and lonely one. The intentionally motherless wife is regarded as defying all the rules and prevailing myths of society—every society. So that even if legislation were passed tomorrow banning the mass media from depicting motherhood as a state of grace—the prevailing practice—the long-gathered pressures to reproduce would hardly vanish and perhaps not even diminish significantly. The lives of millions of women attest that one *can* be fulfilled without bearing children. But until their message and way of life can be presented broadly and honorably, the myth will persevere.

Rationalizations of motherhood are abundant. Babies serve to catch a man, save a marriage, prevent the first child from being lonely, and ensure against loneliness in the parents' old age. But the vast majority of the mothers I spoke with had no reason for having children beyond the feeling that it was natural to have a child at a respectable and reasonable interval following marriage.

But babies are not toys, to be mindlessly acquired. A baby is a human being—a new life. A baby is not a lark to be undertaken because of whim, accident, or social conditioning. And certainly not against the backdrop of untruth about promised fulfillment—a promise that, if it goes unrealized, can lead and has led many a young woman to change her mind about the blessings of motherhood after it is too late.

One would think it a civilized and reasonable thing for a woman to discover *before* the fact whether she is suitable for motherhood. If she's not, the discovery ought to be a source of rejoicing rather than a condition to be overcome or a cause of shame, guilt, or feelings of inadequacy.

Yet there are almost no books or magazines that try to convey to a young woman what it means to be a mother—that tell their readers that the joy and agony, the love and hostility, the pride and the fear are all mingled almost every day; not to understand as much is to risk a traumatic response when the truth is revealed. What Alix Kates Shulman calls "the terrible weight" of motherhood "and the way it affects a woman's personality" has little to do with the drudgery, financial privation, or loss of glamour that accompanies motherhood. It cannot be explained away by the unpleasantness of red hands roughened from swishing diapers in the toilet or by varicose veins or sagging breasts. What cannot be deeply known ahead of time is the never-ending responsibility, the constant demands, and the nerve-shattering crises that characterize the role at least as much as the joys.

The very sight of my children does give me joy, as do so many of the delightful things they do and say and the beautifully absurd presents they make for Mom. These things are very real, and they go straight to a mother's heart. I look at my son and my daughter, and beyond their physical loveliness I see a beauty within them that is breathtaking. They are life. They are everything that is too important and fragile to be treated as casually and insipidly as our culture does through its pervasive dictum that parenthood is universally right and natural for everyone—and oceans of fun.

When I approached motherhood, I did so with enthusiasm and confidence. I felt that my "vast exposure" to children had told me all I needed to know—that I really wanted children and that I was potentially a very good mother. What I hadn't actually learned or known would come naturally during motherhood, I thought. My "vast exposure" to kids consisted mostly of enjoying someone else's children on weekends. We started babysitting for our niece and nephew when we were first married, when they were three and five years old. We made a big thing out of their birthdays and Christmas, took them out on family outings, and looked after them to give their parents a breathing spell—all because we genuinely liked having the kids around.

Seeing these children was easily arranged because they lived right next door to us. They were often hanging around when one or both of us got home from work. But however much we enjoyed having them around, our commitment to them was of course of a different order from the kind parents have to their own youngsters. If I had to run errands when I got home and the kids were there, I'd simply tell them to come back later; if they just wanted to fool around after dinner some night, I could say, "No, you can't come this Friday because we're going out—come Saturday instead." Their parents put in all the work, and we got the gravy. For me they were just two wonderful kids who only added to our lives. We got the part they show on television.

By the time my husband and I had been married for eight years without the patter of little feet under our roof, the friends-relatives-media-society squeeze had done its work at last. I was able to announce to the world that we were no longer irresponsible, hedonistic, immature, abnormal, sterile, frigid, impotent, or homosexual. Good old barren Shirl was very pregnant.

Everyone was overjoyed, including this unsuspecting couple. Everyone was indescribably happy that our life would not prove futile, after all. We were real people. No longer would we feel left out when the talk turned to toilet-training techniques, PTA politics, and orthodontia.

At the time it never occurred to us that we were knuckling under to social pressure. And if it had, I doubt that we would have admitted it. In retrospect, we can see now that it was all around us back then and could not fail to have had a conditioning effect upon us. We never once discussed the matter thoroughly. We never weighed the advantages against the disadvantages because it never occurred to us that we might not be cut out for parenthood—or parenthood for us.

To both of us, having kids when we were ready to have them seemed the most natural thing in the world.

We put more care and thoughtful examination into the purchase of a new automobile than into the decision to bring two lives into the world.

3

The Garden
of Eden

FROM THE MOMENT my doctor revealed the results of my pregnancy test, I was euphoric. That evening, wearing a long, flowing hostess gown, I greeted my husband lovingly, sat us down, and deftly opening a bottle of champagne, proposed a toast to the *three* of us. He did the expected double take and then, in a moment, he was beaming.

While we had hoped to start our family sooner (correcting my faulty thyroid function had taken longer than anticipated), we both agreed that things generally *do* work out for the best. The timing couldn't have been more perfect: We had finished fixing up our little house, we had enough money, and, after eight good years together, our marriage was a solid one. Not only would we bring a wanted child into a secure home, but into one where children truly were cherished. We had a marvelous time surprising everybody with our good news. To our friends in Seattle we said, "Gee, we're sorry we can't come up for a visit this summer, but we've really got to tighten the old belt, settle down, and plan for the future." Then we zonked them with it.

When we were asked whether we wanted a boy or a girl, we gave the answer most happy expectant parents give, "We don't care. We just want a healthy baby."

After things settled down, I set about making sure my unborn child would have the very best. I vowed I would do everything *right* during my pregnancy—it would be to the letter. I picked up a copy of Adelle Davis's *Let's Have Healthy Children* just to make sure my diet would be absolutely right, and religiously followed my doctor's advice to drink one quart of milk each day, eat one serving of meat, and keep the calories down to a thousand a day.

I enrolled in a natural childbirth class, as my obstetrician suggested, and dutifully attended every Wednesday night. The first evening, our instructor, a registered nurse and the mother of three naturally delivered children, gave us a list of books and pamphlets, recommending that we pick them up to understand better what was going on. A perfect instructor, she was young, agile, enthusiastic about both natural childbirth and breast-feeding. She has successfully carried out these methods with all three of her children.

We were told that natural childbirth in a normal pregnancy was fairly easy, provided we did our exercises and learned to relax. Relaxation was the key to success.

We were also told that the value of natural childbirth was that it minimized the use of anesthetics or instruments, which could be harmful to the baby. It was possible to have a virtually painless birth without any anesthetic whatsoever. Our instructor pointed out that the only *real* cause for pain was the episiotomy—the incision that might have to be made to prevent "tearing" at the moment of birth. Usually all that was required for that was a shot of novocain.

The class sat wide-eyed as our instructor told us that she had gotten up off the delivery table after the birth of each of her children and *walked* back to her room.

With the benefits to the baby of natural childbirth and the obvious ease of the natural function, I would, of course, "go Read." I diligently practiced my exercises, learned to pant to maximize relaxation, continued with my good nutrition, and just looked forward happily to the big event.

Some of my classmates were less enthusiastic about their pregnancies; some suffered from morning sickness (I never had a twinge). Some of my pregnant friends would actually go on starvation diets the week before they went to see their doctors just to avoid the disapproval. "Tsk, tsk, they are only fooling themselves," said I, having no trouble with *my* weight.

One of my classmates who was depressed over her "planned pregnancy" confessed that she would eat to excess and then get depressed over her weight gain. Another friend quit her job early in her pregnancy and spent seven months telling everyone how bored she was. My friend Lynn had morning sickness for four months, overate at the drop of a hat, and confessed to me that she wasn't at all sure she should have gotten pregnant so soon in her marriage.

My only concern rested with preparing to be a really super mother to my baby, and so while some of my less fortunate pregnant friends seemed disturbed about being pregnant, I busied myself with learning all I could about delivery and child care.

Our classes had been under way for about four weeks when a representative of the LaLeche League came around to give a lecture. LaLeche, a national organization with chapters in many cities, exists solely to educate expectant mothers about the benefits and techniques of breast-feeding their babies, to help new mothers who are experiencing difficulties in nursing, and to supply mother's milk in emergency situations. Their numerous spokeswomen educate the public and a large volunteer "work force" of experienced nursing mothers stands ready to go out and help new mothers having breast-feeding problems —a new mother has only to call her local chapter, and a member comes round to help. Our lecturer that evening told the class that mother's milk is much more nutritious than formula and that it even provides a baby with immunities against infection. Then she described her own experiences. Her baby had been delivered naturally and the birth had been totally painless. Her husband had accompanied her to the delivery room, where together they watched the birth of their child in a large overhead mirror. It was the most beautiful experience of her life. Then she told us of the joy of caring for her baby in her hospital room instead of leaving him in the nursery. (Some hospitals make such provision for new mothers who, with the help of a nurse, take over the care of their newborns; they feed them, diaper them, and assume almost all maternal responsibilities right from the beginning.) Our LaLeche spokeswoman described breast-feeding, echoing the words of Niles Newton:

> Successful breast feeding is so easy! It is simply a matter of holding a hungry baby to the breast and relaxing and letting him suck. Nature does the rest. The more milk the baby takes out of the breast, the more milk the body puts back into the breast. . . .[1]

and assured the class that "anyone who truly *wants* to nurse her baby can do so—it is, after all, the *natural* way to do things."

The lecture reinforced my decision to breast-feed my child. There had never been any real doubt because I wanted to do everything right. And now I had even more proof that breast feeding was natural, easy, good for a new mother, and *so* good for the baby.

When my obstetrician asked me if I would be nursing the baby, I responded enthusiastically and affirmatively. He wagged a very long index finger in my face and said, "Okay—but plan to bottle-feed, too. Otherwise you won't be able to get away from the baby for any length of time."

"But doctor, why would I want to leave my own baby for more than four hours?"

During the last two months of what was a fine and easy pregnancy, I got even more serious about the impending arrival. My husband was delighted. He often referred to my "nesting instinct." With joy and love and beautiful new baby furniture, I put the nursery together. But it didn't stop at the baby's room. I tore our house apart, gave it a thorough cleaning, repainted the interior, rearranged the furniture, shampooed the carpet, stripped and waxed floors, washed and ironed curtains, and packed my suitcase. I organized kitchen cabinets for the babythings, and cleaned out my sewing cupboard to use it for the higher purpose of storing baby clothes.

I continued to read my books, do my exercises, go to classes, and practice going with the contractions or labor pains, and panting. About a month before the baby was due, I went on a tour of the hospital so I'd know where everything was, and, more importantly, where my husband was to take me when the time came. During the tour, along with about thirty other pregnant women, I saw even more films concerning the miracle of birth and child care and received a free gift packet of all manner of things, including formula that this new mother would never need.

At shortly after 10 P.M. on February 17, 1965, the contractions started coming at regular intervals, and I was pretty certain that I'd be a mother before morning. After talking to my doctor and being assured that I wouldn't somehow magically deliver the baby while sleeping (so relaxed and prepared was I), I went to bed.

At 3:15 A.M. on February 18, I nudged my husband and told him to wake up, get himself together, and take me to the hospital.

Once we got settled in the labor room, the contractions started coming furiously, and they were *hard*. I hadn't expected such intense pain, and I kept trying to go with it, employing the breathing technique I had learned in the class and faithfully practiced. My husband had never seen me in any pain, and he was obviously disturbed.

It isn't unusual for a first-timer to have intense pain, but to someone standing on the sidelines it can look scary —particularly if that someone has been assured by his wife that all her preparation was going to make matters move along simply and painlessly. While my husband looked forward to the baby, there was no way that he would have traded his wife of eight years for an infant he didn't know yet. The labor room scene put that kind of question to him. It also introduced something else.

I forgot all about him. When my doctor came in to assess the situation, he took one look and ordered a sedative for me. While I was going down for the count, I asked him if I'd be able to do everything naturally. I was concerned only about the delivery of my child. I was asleep before I caught his answer.

The sedative had an interesting effect. I would sleep soundly between contractions, waking up only while the pain lasted, and then immediately drop off. My first tiny failure at being The Perfect New Mother came when I welcomed the anesthetic. I wasn't going to "go Read" after all. While suffering body-wracking contractions and genuinely wanting relief, I felt disappointed and ashamed that I didn't have the stuff to do it naturally. (The instructor in my class had said. "Anyone who really *wants* to, *can*.")

I thought of the other women in my class and wondered jealously how many of them were going to be able to do easily what I couldn't. And I remembered the woman who came to class after having a baby a few days before: she described the birth as one so easy "they almost didn't get me to the hospital on time." Then, after feeling maternal inadequacy for the first time and setting aside my concern for my wounded vanity, I had my first taste of maternal fear and guilt. I started worrying about what effect the anesthetic or instruments would have on the baby—and if forceps would be required to help my "unnatural" delivery—they could be harmful also. My baby wasn't even here and I'd let him down already.

Shortly after the production started, it was over. At 9:15 A.M., I was the mother of the most beautiful baby girl I'd ever seen. My fears and guilt over not having natural childbirth were forgotten when I first saw Lisa. I thought I'd explode with joy as I looked at her. Petal pink, lots of black hair and lovely eyelashes, and oh, so tiny and perfect. Later that day, hand in hand, my husband and I walked to the nursery and stood transfixed, looking at our lovely baby through the glass.

We were enchanted. I thought for a moment about my friend Barbara who had confessed that she didn't feel anything for her new baby. How terribly sad. Barbara's pregnancy had been as easy as mine. She was working when she got pregnant, kept working until a month before the baby was due, glowed all through it. When I visited her, the baby was about two months old. She said she was desperately tired, couldn't stand the work of taking care of a baby, and saw the baby only as something that was turning her into a miserable machine. Barbara said that she felt unnatural—why hadn't she felt a rush of love for the baby when she first saw her, and why hadn't she felt it yet? She was ashamed to admit her feelings even to her husband.

When we finally broke the spell of gazing silently through the glass and returned to my room, our talk was only of Lisa. I had not yet held her in my arms, and I was itching to get my hands on her. Cal envied me: "You'll at least get to be with her here, but I have to wait until I take you home." But that was just another sign that my husband fully shared my joy and instant love. When I held Lisa in my arms for the first time, I didn't want ever to let her go. They took her back to the nursery much too soon but I was comforted by knowing that, since I was nursing her, I'd get to be with her every four hours. When they asked me if I wanted to be awakened for the 2 A.M. and 6 A.M. feedings, I answered, "Absolutely."

During our hospital stay, I lived from one feeding time to the next and for the two visiting periods when I would get to see Cal. He was growing increasingly eager for us to leave the hospital. Me, too. It was time for us to start being a real family.

It was wonderful to be home. Lisa went to sleep nicely and we enjoyed a quiet dinner, alone together for the first time in nearly a week. After dinner, I reviewed some material on breast-feeding and infant care until it was time for another feeding. Things went beautifully, and I noted with pride that I had lots of milk. Taking care of Lisa was going to be a snap. When one of the doctors saw my baby for the first time, he asid, "Boy, are you going to have fun —taking care of her is going to be just like playing dolls."

By the time the 10 P.M. feeding rolled around, both mother and baby were so relaxed that, moments afterward, both were sound asleep.

The next day, Cal went to work, and Lisa and I were on our own. I was a little anxious about taking care of her without any help, but I was feeling marvelous and, after all, mothering *was* natural and as old as the human race.

When Cal got home, he was great. He spent most of that second evening at home holding her and giving me encouragement. It had been a good and easy day, but it was nice to have company and moral support.

After she'd had her six o'clock feeding, we just enjoyed having Lisa with us for a time, and then we reluctantly agreed we should put her to bed. We might as well have simply moved the cradle into the living room because it seemed as if one of us were checking on her constantly. It started out by our going in to take an extra little look at her; as the evening progressed, we realized that we were actually monitoring her.

On one occasion Cal caught me in the act. I was pinching Lisa's foot gently. My explanation—"I just wanted to make sure she was still breathing. She was awfully still" —met with stern disapproval. I caught him doing the same thing the next night.

We agreed that this sort of hovering about was going to make the baby nervous and reassured each other that she would be just fine—in fact, as Cal said, she would probably be greatly relieved that we quit pestering her.

Two weeks after her birth, our precious little girl started losing weight, and I panicked. I called the pediatrician. By the time we got there, Lisa was weak and rapidly becoming ill. The doctor weighed her and gave her a thorough examination, and then asked me if I were still breast-feeding. After I said yes, he said, "She's starving," and instructed me to start feeding her formula right away. He told me my milk had apparently dried up and suggested that if I gave her formula and continued putting her to my breast, my milk might come in again.

In a matter of days Lisa was thriving, and I was nearly back to my normal happy state. But before that, I was scared, disgusted, and ashamed. I had put my child through this misery to prove a point, to satisfy my own vanity; in an effort to be The Most Perfect Mother, I'd nearly starved our baby. I felt so very inadequate. I had let my child down by not being able to give her all the benefits of mother's milk. And I had compounded the failure—no, *crime*—by being too dumb and too vain to realize what was really going on.

I'd like to take this opportunity to thank the LaLeche League for really driving home the syndrome of fear and guilt—right at the onset of my motherhood. I'd also like to thank some competitive new mothers I knew in those days—the ones I asked for advice when I suspected something might be wrong. The ones who answered me with, "I don't know. I never had any problems. It's just a natural thing."

Ah but, LaLeche, you didn't leave my life quite yet. One day after I'd acknowledged that I was a dismal failure on more than one count, you made contact once again through the miracle of television. I was just about to feed Lisa, so I switched on the TV while she enthusiastically did away with her formula. There you were on a morning women's talk show, one of your ardent troops firing up the audience with a speech: "Breast-feeding is so easy, fulfilling, good for the baby, and good for Mother, too! When my baby gains weight, I know that *I* did that—I'm responsible for the fact that he is thriving. That's *my* own accomplishment—I did it all by myself. Any woman who loves her child can do the same."

I only recently pondered the pervasive attitude that says any woman can, if she wants to, which leads to the illogical conclusion that when a young mother can't earn her marks either in the delivery room or with successful suckling, it's because she is somehow inadequate, shallow, or loves her child less than her friends who can.

If breast-feeding is so easy to bring off, then why is there a need for a whole organization, with chapters virtually everywhere, to help women accomplish through instruction and encouragement what is "so natural" and so easy? If it's that easy, why does Dr. Spock devote nine pages to the problems of breast-feeding? How does Niles Newton's description of the ease and simplicity of breast-feeding reconcile with the following eleven pages, which describe the many difficulties that can surface? [2]

Breast-feeding may well be very easy for some mothers —maybe most. But that fact should not be used as a club to coerce new mothers into feeling that they must adopt the method or brand those who don't or can't as dismal failures. It's not a *great* failure—but in its present cultist context, it is not of the early, unnecessary ones that can start the ball rolling for the inadequacy trip that each new day of motherhood can bring.

Some mothers who have nursed quite successfully never really wanted to. One such mother said to me, "Of course I breast-fed my child—I had to—all my friends did, and I couldn't be a misfit, could I?" Still another admitted, "I hated it— I was trapped by the baby. Being successful at it doesn't mean you'll like it." Another woman who disdained the fad fanfare, said, "Personally, it didn't make much difference to me. I did it for the baby."

Summing up the pressures on expectant and new mothers to do everything naturally—and therefore the right way—one woman said, "Thank God, I had to have a Caesarean. It gave me a marvelous excuse for not having natural childbirth, which I didn't want that much in the first place. Having the decision taken out of my hands made me feel less guilty about not doing it for the baby, and I could hold up my head in front of my pro-natural-childbirth friends."

Lisa was a wonderful baby, and the three of us got along beautifully. I'd weathered the breast-feeding storm, and then an interesting thing happened. I ran out of powdered formula, but I had some liquid formula that I'd brought home from the hospital. Everything went swimmingly, but the baby's bowel patterns changed radically. I couldn't imagine why. Babies have lots of bowel movements every day, so I didn't notice an unusual increase until after about three days when it started getting worse. Then she developed a diaper rash. This, of course, made her very fussy, and made me feel that I was doing something wrong—maybe the laundry, or maybe I wasn't changing her often enough or using the right powders and lotions. As the diaper rash got worse, she became fussier,

I became more upset and guilty about whatever it was I was doing, and we seemed to be caught in another downhill cycle. I called the pediatrician and reported the changes in her bowel patterns, and he seemed unperturbed. Then I called and discussed the diaper rash, and he made a few suggestions. I tried them all.

Monday we trotted over to the doctor. "Lisa has diarrhea. That's why she's dehydrated and has a diaper rash," was the pediatrician's proclamation. Then he asked if I'd introduced any new foods or juices in the baby's diet, or if any changes had taken place. I assured him that I had followed all of his instructions to the letter. Finally, bewildered, he wrote out a prescription for something that would stop the diarrhea and said, "She's not really sick. Not yet, anyway, but diarrhea can be debilitating. Already she's lost a little weight, and we can't have that."

Lisa was marvelous through it all. Sure she was fussy, but she was still cheerful and sweet, and surprisingly, she slept through the night.

The next morning when I got her up for a diaper change and her "breakfast," she still was having the same old problems. For the next few days, the diarrhea lessened, but it didn't clear up. I called the pediatrician; he was genuinely puzzled, and we agreed that I should bring her in again.

That evening while I was fixing dinner, I started rearranging the cupboard where I kept the baby things—I suppose in an effort to keep as busy as possible and thereby subdue my fears about Lisa. I was putting away the new cans of powdered formula I had picked up that day and was considering our dilemma when suddenly a light went on. There was something wrong with the formula I had been using. I had switched from powder to liquid, using the same brand. That was the change in her diet. It wasn't even a real change because it was supposed to be the same stuff in a more convenient form.

Lisa dear, for the first time in your young life your incompetent mother did something right. She dumped all the liquid down the drain, made a whole new batch of powdered formula, told a dismayed pediatrician that she was a lucky genius, and progressively started compensating for a month of hell.

In three days, Lisa started looking like a real baby again—a little thin, but healthier. Her diarrhea and diaper rash were over, for the most part, and our trip to paradise was rescheduled and starting. As I came up from a month of feeling greater terror than I had ever felt in my life, a level of inadequacy and guilt never before imagined, I pondered a question: Is original sin meant to be regarded as innate in man as a direct result of Adam's sin? Or maybe it got garbled in the translation, and it is really the shame felt by a new mother when she commits her first innocent sin against her new child.

4

The joys of parenthood

"GOOD GOD, SHIRL, are you sure? What will people *think?* Lisa isn't even five months old, and pretty soon you'll be busting out all over."

I wasn't only sure, I was delighted. Once I had gotten over the rough spots of taking care of Lisa—the fear and guilt of our bad beginnings nearly forgotten—I'd thoroughly enjoyed her. Our little girl had become such a delight that I was certain that another baby would only add to our happiness. I assured my self-conscious husband that people would only think good thoughts, and hardly think we were sex maniacs. "After all, Cal, people *do* get together after they have a baby. No one's going to think we've been behaving like impetuous teenagers. Everyone's going to think it's great."

And they did. Everyone expressed joy that we would have another baby soon. Many of our friends told us how relieved they were that we were not going to burden Lisa with being an only child. And there was much talk of the good genes that couldn't help but produce another lovely child.

Caring for Lisa and the house had become such a simple routine that I felt certain another baby wouldn't complicate matters. If things continued as beautifully with Lisa, and I brought the experience of her early babyhood to a second child, having two kids would be just as easy as having one.

In many ways I was quite correct. The months with Lisa before our next child was born were a breeze; she was almost never ill, she wasn't fussy, and she was loads of fun. She was a beautiful, healthy baby. She had a sense of humor, and she was busy discovering her world; just looking at her or being with her provided reason to have another baby. She became more delightful each day and easier to care for. And every day we loved her more. She learned to crawl and started to investigate every corner of the house, but her Mom was way ahead of her. I totally child-proofed our house.

Like my first pregnancy, my second was perfect. No morning sickness, no aches and pains, no incredible weight gains. I didn't attend classes this time because I'd done that and I knew pretty much what to expect. Instead, I went out and looked for a larger house. I found one that was ideal for a growing young family. There were three large bedrooms, two modern baths, and an enormous all-electric kitchen with room for everything including play-pens. We left our tiny palace with reluctance—it was our first home, however small and inconvenient; we had put it together ourselves and we had shared many happy, loving hours there.

My second baby was due on Valentine's Day. The day before, my father searched the San Francisco peninsula to find just the right gift for me, and then he proudly delivered it. He found a *blue* Valentine heart, and he gave it to me with these words. "This is to hope that you'll even it out and have a boy. It's nice to have one of each."

Hi, Dr. Lamaze; Hi, Dr. Read. Guess what I just did? I just had a natural delivery. Know why? Because I had stretched my undersized birth canal just a year before. That's why.

One hour after we had arrived at the hospital, Cal and I were having breakfast together in my room and calling friends and family. My parents were flabbergasted when I got on the line and said, "We just had a son a few minutes ago—his name is Adam."

Adam was born on Monday, February 14—right on

73

schedule—and on Wednesday morning we were being tossed out of the hospital because everyone seemed hale and hardy and they needed my bed.

When we got home, I prepared dinner in advance, got Adam settled, made formula (no way was I going to put this kid through what Lisa suffered), breast-fed him for a while, backed it up with a bottle, and then called my sister who had kindly kept Lisa while I was in the hospital. When she indicated that they would happily keep her for a few days, I said, "No, I've missed my little girl and I want her home."

Adam is different from Lisa in many ways. A mother conjures up images of what her baby will look like, and I had based the image of my second baby on what Lisa looked like at birth. But instead Adam was a blond baby, and beautifully so. To this day his hair is as white as paper, his skin very fair, and he has enormous deep-blue eyes. He's adorable—but in a way much different from Lisa. They're both beautiful and healthy and wonderful. But they look so fascinatingly different.

When we brought Adam home and greeted our baby daughter, we were prepared for still another pleasant and uneventful year, particularly since I wasn't about to make the same mistakes with this baby as I had with my first— I had learned too much the hard way.

The birth of my daughter just a year before had introduced me to the genuine joy of motherhood—it had also introduced me to the sting of failure that hurts so much when you really want to do everything as well as the rest of the gang—just as well, that is, as they tell you they did. But more important, a new mother wants to do everything right for the baby.

Adam was about to introduce me to another dimension of parental joy, but before he could do so, his sister put my stomach in my shoes.

On the day we brought Adam home from the hospital our one-year-old baby girl dived head first off her changing table. With Mom standing right there. I had been restraining her with one hand and reaching for a diaper with the other, when I felt her slip. Suddenly she was on the floor and she wasn't crying—a fact I didn't notice right off because little Adam was very loudly exercising his lungs. I scooped Lisa up and started crying while I was leafing through my Dr. Spock to check for symptoms of concussion. It's amazing how many different thoughts the human mind is capable of handling simultaneously. While looking for the appropriate section in the book, I was yelling to my husband to call the pediatrician, rocking Lisa and feeling a rush of terrible guilt that she had slipped from my grasp. And fear! My God, was I scared! I was convinced that I was the only mother who ever even *suspected* her one-year-old baby had sustained a concussion. The pediatrician assured us that Lisa would be just fine. "These things happen all the time," he said. How comforting to know that I could look forward to a whole string of things like that.

As soon as we had recovered from our near hysteria over Lisa, we noticed that Adam breathed funny. We listened as he rasped away, wondering to each other what in the world could be wrong. Then a strange thing happened. He choked and then vomited up some mucus. I didn't know what to make of it, so naturally I called the pediatrician. He assured us it was nothing, that normally this mucus is expelled while the baby is still in the hospital but that not infrequently it took a little longer. What a relief! Now he would breathe normally.

But he didn't. Not then, and not six months from then. We found ourselves behaving with him much as we had with Lisa, when we used to hover around her while she was sleeping. If he didn't make that strange noise, we thought he had drawn his last breath. For months I feared that one morning I would wake up and find a dead baby in the cradle. The first night Adam slept clear through, instead of waking up refreshed from an uninterrupted sleep, I jumped out of bed in a panic to see if he were still alive.

I found his breathing not only unnerving, but a source of almost constant anxiety—an undercurrent that was always there. Always. That edge of fear that his respiratory system would fail.

As had happened with Lisa, each day Adam was with us our love for him deepened, and he brought his own sparkle to the family. As my love for him grew, so did my concern and my realization that now that he was here, life would be unbearable without him.

Adam's next contribution to my education (in things not mentioned by those who say how much fun parenthood is) was noise. Unlike Lisa, who cried for a reason, he just cried.

He cried and I worried. He cried loudly, urgently, and most of the time. If he cried because he was hungry, he would just continue while he was eating, after he was finished, and after he was burped.

I thought there must be something wrong with him. Maybe it had something to do with his strange breathing. But the doctor could not find anything wrong—not even colic. So I worried. And Adam cried.

It is not just that it is difficult to hear above all the racket; it is difficult to think even simple thoughts. With Adam's constant crying, I found it difficult to do anything more complicated than heat his bottle; closing a pin on a diaper became a major technical feat. On one occasion he cried incessantly because he had a diaper rash—I accepted his noise as my penalty for maternal incompetence, until my sympathy (very real in the beginning) deteriorated into anger.

Occasionally when it got bad, I would put Adam in his crib and go sit outside. The trade-off was a few moments of peace and quiet for the guilty feeling that I was being indifferent to my baby's troubles.

One of the dubious joys of parenthood is learning that you are capable of feeling annoyed at a tiny innocent baby. Sometimes I would hear myself saying, "You're not being *fair*. Here I am trying to take care of you, do *your* laundry, and make a nice home for *you,* and this is how I'm treated," to two kids whose vocabularies consisted of "gurgle" and "da," respectively.

Trailing closely behind petty feelings like that was the constant fear that somewhere along the line I *was* doing something wrong, but just couldn't figure out what it might be.

During one of Adam's stormy sessions. I had something I'll loosely term a telephone conversation with another mother. Adam was screaming at the top of his lungs when she called. Her voice was being drowned out by the strains of another baby at her end of the line. "How's it going?" I asked. She told me.

"After listening to ten solid hours of an infant crying, my nerves are shot, and if I didn't have the responsibility of taking care of this baby, I swear I'd get drunk." What little voice she had left broke while she talked. She had consulted their pediatrician, who assured her there was nothing wrong with the child—just a little indigestion. "Don't worry, Mrs. Smith, the baby is just fine."

Comforting words like that go a long way toward relieving a mother's concern for her child; they say nothing of how to alleviate the suffering of a mother who is slowly being driven out of her mind.

"You know," my friend continued, "when it first starts I really feel sorry for Cindy because I know she hurts. But after it goes on interminably, I just get nervous and tired and sometimes I don't even like her. And then I feel horrible about feeling that way." To my suggestion that she ask her mother to help out she said. "That's not really fair —she's more than willing, but why should I put it on her?"

Monday-morning quarterbacking—the pious "yes, buts" and "if onlys"—helps neither a fussy baby nor a mother in absolute agony, nerves taut, bathed in guilt. Someone is always hanging around in the wings with advice like, "The baby cries a lot because she doesn't get enough love," or, "If you'd breast-feed the baby she wouldn't get indigestion." If breast-feeding dispels the breast-feeding friend another crops up who suggests: "The breast-feeding is probably the *cause* of the baby's problem."

When my friend Alice's baby had colic, absolutely

77

everyone had an opinion about the cause. The opinions boiled down to one: Good mothers don't have bad babies. That was a great help as she sat at the kitchen table, her head in her arms, sobbing her heart out, while her child continued to wail. This perfectly healthy young woman with a fine strong baby ultimately became so exhausted and overwrought that she started hemorrhaging.

One woman could readily have afforded to deposit her baby with a sitter or hire a nurse to come in. She said there were times when she detested the "thing" generating all that noise. Yet she didn't have the heart to leave him with a nurse while he was feeling so terrible.

To know your child is in pain is agony. To know you can't do a damn thing about it makes it worse; it isn't possible to get your mind off the problem while your nerve endings are being ravaged by the sound of loud wails.

It is quite possible for the tenderest and most loving mother to feel absolute hatred for a child who has been making that terrible noise for hours on end. She can hardly be rational after listening to that, knowing she can neither leave it nor turn it off. It should hardly be necessary to add that the most intelligent mothers find it confusing to hate someone they love who is in pain. It should hardly be necessary to point out that they feel guilty and unnatural when they do. It is hardly an unusual way to feel.

As the children grow, the strains of caring for young babies are replaced gradually by other trivia and different crises. The constantly crying baby turns into a toddler who cries only a "normal" amount from bumps on the head, cut knees, and being said "no" to. That diaper changes become less frequent provides the extra time a mother needs to clean up messes, sweep up piles of glass that once may have been lovely vases, and follow her child around ensuring that he doesn't destroy himself in the process of destroying the house.

The first order of business when a mother notices that her infant is becoming a crawler, and will soon be a toddler, is to child-proof the house. That proved to be my forte. All sharp objects, breakable items, potential poisons, and table lighters were put away. The electric range had all of the controls at the back—out of the reach of children. Pens, pencils, sewing gear were tucked so far away that even *I* had trouble getting to them.

Not only was I efficient and diligent in making our home a safe one for children, but I was efficient about my household routine, structuring it around my children's naps. I was extremely well organized, and I found that the drudgery associated with caring for young children was really not as bad as I had anticipated.

Cleaning house, while tedious and boring, is a pretty straightforward business—a matter of getting a good routine and sticking to it. But the sticking-to-it part gets increasingly difficult as the little ones spend less time sleeping and more time getting into mischief, until doing the housework, laundry, writing checks to pay bills, and preparing meals can seem formidable tasks to a mother with young children. The children must come first. An unmade bed cannot compete with a hungry child or a child in trouble, or one who just needs a little love and attention at a given time.

To illustrate the frustration associated with homemaking and caring for young kids:

The day starts on a bright note, with the delightful sight of six-year-old Adam, hair as white as the pages of this book, amazingly beautiful, blue devilish eyes, and a funny grin missing two teeth. Beside this vision of a mother's dream is still another dream: Sweet Lisa, so-dubbed because it fits. She is beautiful, adorable, and fascinating. When I open my eyes in the morning, the sight of these two—so healthy, so bright, so funny—never fails to stir my deepest and finest emotions.

From this delicious beginning, it is inconceivable that the average day would ultimately give way to hostility, resentment, and absolute fury. But the schizophrenic facts are in, for this mother at least, and I have learned, and I hope adjusted to, the knowledge that although I adore Adam and Lisa, and can be totally pleased by the sight of them when I first wake up, by six o'clock that same evening I can feel like heaving them through a plate glass window.

The first discordant note begins with our difference of opinion about bathroom togetherness. I don't like it. My husband doesn't like it. The kids insist on it. My firmness in the matter is generally rewarded with semiprivacy, and while I'm inside, they bang on the door, whine, talk, scuffle with each other, and ask questions while the water is running. Gathering up all of my Dr. Spock-inspired parental sense, I reason with them, and after a few minutes I realize that although my normal speaking voice has risen several decibels, my volume isn't sufficient to beat out the competition.

With the bathroom ordeal out of the way, I trudge to the kitchen to see about breakfast. While putting it all together, breakfast-wise, they are taking it all apart, kitchen-wise. While my hands and eyes are occupied with the dangerous practice of cooking around children, they are occupied with crawling on the drainboard, getting into the cookie jar, running the water, and helping me as much as possible ("but Mommy, I want to help"). As soon as I'm safely extricated from the cooking process, I again draw on the wit and wisdom of Dr. Spock, and coax them off the drainboard and encourage them to enjoy breakfast.

After the routine argument about who sits where, their father makes his appearance, surveys the mess and chaos, and grunts his irritation. We begin.

Once they start eating, they are very serious, and very quiet. It's toward the end of any meal that things get into full swing—gargling with their milk, chewing vigorously with mouths open wide (or, as they would say to each other, "showing your food"), laughing, pounding, shouting, and whatever else can be contrived to annoy, while we try to point out that this behavior is rude and unacceptable. No one hears. The theme has many variations. For example:

1. The gargling, chewing, etc., continues, and Adam chokes. This is very frightening, but he's been doing it for five years now. I pick him up, turn him upside

80

down, and he works it out (so to speak). The rest is easy—Mom cleans up the mess.

2. The gargling and other nonsense continue, Lisa continues her thing, and Adam simply vomits on the breakfast table.
3. Dad reinforces Spock with a yardstick.
4. Mom reinforces Spock with a yardstick.

Then we get dressed. The ritual consists of Lisa crying that her favorite dress of the week is in the hamper. Somehow, we always find an adequate substitute, and she acquiesces through tears. While this is going on, Adam is putting his shirt on backwards, and because he put his shoes on first, the next hurdle requires getting on his Levi's over his shoes. No success to date, and no diminishing amount of loud anguish on his part. We finally get everyone who is going anywhere dressed, combed, washed, and brushed—and on school days, to the bus stop with no time to spare.

Now that Adam and Lisa are in school, once I get through the morning routine, I have four hours to myself each weekday. Well, not exactly—I have four hours to clean house, plan meals, do laundry, keep appointments, go to the school (more on that later), and do what I'm doing right now. Weekends and vacations, however, are very reminiscent of the pre-school days; certainly no description of motherhood would be complete without discussing what it's like when the kids are home all day. It goes like this:

After breakfast has been gotten through somehow, I do the dishes, make the beds, and load the washer. Then I manage to get dressed and see to the numerous household chores. Interspersed with scrubbing a floor, making a bed, and whatever, are demands for Mother that range from getting a glass of water to rushing a bleeding child to the doctor. I can start simply: The water is running. It's in the bathroom. No, it's in the garage. Then there is the sudden realization that it's both places, and you can only manage one at a time. They've got you at either end of the house. Or: You hear crying. It's Adam. No, it's Lisa. No, it's both. Are they hurt? Who is hurt worse? Who needs the most immediate attention? Sometimes there is a chorus of other kids going all at once. This seems a good place to note that the mother of two children very often supervises four, five, or six kids all at once—they're called playmates. Or:

You are retrieving your purse from the toilet, wondering which of the little darlings put it there, and you have a funny feeling. It feels less funny when you remove the laundry from the dryer and discover that your best permanent-press clothes were dried with your new lipstick tossed in by innocent hands. Or:

You are comforting a hurt child, putting a Band-Aid on a knee or inspecting a bumped head—you hear a crash in another part of the house or yard, and you are once again pulled apart by the simultaneous needs of both of your children. One is high in a tree and the other is climbing on the roof . . . and so it goes.

And all the while you are trying to get through the drudgery, and suffering the continuous, simultaneous, child-generated chaos, there are the never-ending requests for water, food, cookies, Scotch tape, paper, and anything else they think they want. Now toss in the constant battles that inevitably accompany siblings close in age.

Somewhere in the course of the average day, lunch time is signaled by the appearance of Adam and Lisa with three friends. They have invited these friends for lunch. We then have a private chat. We go over the business of inviting friends to lunch without first asking Mom if it's all right, and then compound the error by asking in front of said friends while the friends stand around looking hungry. If they are denied these guests, there are two broken hearts, tears, and shouts of "You don't love us."

After lunch (friends and all), we return to more of the same, punctuated with interruptions by students selling magazine subscriptions, more playmates at the door, scouts selling candy, Fuller Brush men, Avon ladies, and phone calls telling me that we've just won a full-color photo of the kiddies for only six dollars and when will we be coming to the studio?

This brings us up to dinner time.

The National Safety Council tells us that the majority of home accidents take place in the early evening while mothers are preparing dinner. If I haven't gotten a head start earlier in the day, cooking becomes a major feat. The children are hungry, curious, talkative, and constantly underfoot. And Mom is usually pretty tired at this point. *This has to be the worst part of the day.*

Dinner is a repeat, with some variation, of breakfast and lunch. Usually this is when I hear I'm a terrible cook, the food I serve is just "icky," and that Jeffie's Mom serves "real good hamburgers" every night.

After dinner, there is television for a while, followed by the usual argument about taking a bath. After that is settled, they have their bath, sloshing water on the walls, the floor, the ceiling, and Mom when she checks on them.

Cal and I finally get them dried and combed, all teeth brushed, and coaxed into their pajamas, and then we go through the routine debate about going to bed. That settled, they are kissed and tucked into bed and go to sleep so quickly one wonders why they argued about it. *This has to be the best time of the day.*

Once the kids are asleep, we enjoy an hour or two of "leisure" when we can both read, work, or listen to music without interruption. When I don't work during that period it's generally because I'm too tired, and very often I wind up just going to bed or falling asleep huddled over the typewriter or sitting in a chair.

On the nights that I last as long as my husband, staying up the extra hour or so, we look in on the children before we fall into the sack ourselves. We've nearly always done this. There is something about sleeping children that allows parents a special look. Perhaps it's a catching-up time for parents like us. We can truly enjoy them without engaging in battle; we overcome the tribulations of the day. Who knows? This is the time we see them not solely as our charges but as Adam and Lisa—two very lovely children—and the sight of them never fails to stir the finest emotions a parent will know.

It could be said that there is nothing unique about the

daily routine I've just described. That is precisely the point. There is nothing unique about it.

I have discussed my routine with my own children for the sake of completeness—to outline for the uninitiated what the *least* of that routine is all about—but it is only a brief outline. However, even the most detailed account of the drudgery and confusion involved in caring for kids would not speak of the real gut issues of parenthood.

When society speaks to us about the joys of parenthood it leaves out a hell of a lot far more important than drudgery and confusion (But still the trivia is almost never part of the picture presented to young adults, and these trivial pitfalls can come as a surprise to many new parents.) If the drudgery is glossed over by society in its hot pursuit of turning every young married adult into a parent, that sin of omission pales next to the failure to tell the truth about far more serious matters.

Parenthood can be a lot of work, the associated drudgery can be boring as hell, the rewards can be minimal, and the terrors associated with caring for an infant when inexperienced very serious. But it doesn't end there. That is only a tiny beginning—the first deposit in the negative bank account of accumulated disappointments, fears, guilts, and inadequacies a mother feels.

How unbelievably petty my routine sounds. And yet, life is made up of small things. Taken one by one, each frustration or annoyance is as nothing, but the opportunities for all the feelings of guilt and inadequacy are there.

(Am I letting them watch TV too much because I want them out of the way? Will anything bad happen if I don't bathe them for three days because I can't face the fight? How could I possibly have let myself not brush their hair? Am I being a dreadful mother because I let them have candy before dinner? Is dinner nutritious enough? Will they starve or grow up anemic because I can't face the hassle of shoving food down their little throats?) And through all this runs the thread of responsibility. Every action, every act of discipline, every Frito given or not given is contributing to what they will become. Am I doing it right or wrong? And how can I remain reasonable when the petty frustrations seem to be destroying my ability to reason? And, if I find the job for all the reasons an unpleasant one, am I a bad mother?

The annoyance of simultaneously scrubbing a toilet and being nagged by a child cannot be compared to the fear and inadequacy one feels when a child is hurt or sick. I have described concussion in a one-year-old, but getting through that didn't prepare me for future incidents—no mother can be so prepared; instead, she only becomes more sensitive and sensitized by the dangers as time passes.

Louise, for example, a very cautious mother, sadly learned that her efficiency nearly cost her both her children. Louise had completely child-proofed her house, putting all medications and cleaning compounds in a locked suitcase on the top shelf of her closet. Her children wouldn't be able to ingest a lethal dose of anything. At least not in *her* house. But when a babysitter carelessly left allergy medicine on a counter, she learned that you can *never* be too sure. She didn't know it was in the house until she found the empty bottle. Suddenly the children's listlessness that morning took on a new meaning. She got in touch with her pediatrician, who said, "You can't take any chances. They may not have taken anything, then again they may have—and if vomiting doesn't bring anything up, we'll have to pump their stomachs."

Louise was lucky. She had moved swiftly enough so that the vomiting did the trick. "They had taken enough to put them to sleep permanently," she told me, "and the fear I felt at the time and sympathy for the two I was forcing to vomit is indescribable. To say nothing of the guilt."

"Oh, but that won't happen to *me,*" you might be saying. "That only happens occasionally." Really? Statistics indicate that during 1972, 500,000 children ingested lethal amounts of medication, cleaning solvents, and other poisons.

Careful and cautious mothers are scarcely immune. No

85

one ever knows precisely what the neighbors are up to. The family with the prettiest yard on the block, for example, may be a menace to your child. A friend of mine reported that her two-year-old ate a poisoned snail that had crawled over from a neighbor's yard. Our next door neighbor came rushing over one day to report that he had been spraying with dangerous pesticides and Adam had gone into the yard to retrieve his ball. I immediately took my son into the house, lathered him up, and scrubbed him from head to foot, and worried about the incident for days —because two days later our small dog died from pesticide poisoning, and I found dead baby birds on our patio.

One day, Adam disappeared. The police combed the area for one agonizing hour before he was found by some neighborhood boys. He was only three years old; one minute he was in our fenced back yard, and the next minute— gone! I was terrified.

I could write volumes on what my children have either done or the dangers to which they have been exposed, the sort of things you don't think about when you don't have kids. For example, one father pointed out that he had never thought much about hammers until he saw his two-year-old with one—the little boy was ready to hit his four-year-old brother on the head. A mother tells of her little boy running into the house with his head bleeding. It seems that he and a playmate were digging in the back yard. She had no idea where they got a pick ax, but they did, and a fight broke out. The result was a visit to the emergency ward.

Many more volumes could be provided by every mother I have ever met. How many near misses all of our kids have had while riding their bikes? How many of us have cringed as our children have chased toys or pets into the path of oncoming cars?

Somehow, most kids survive. At what cost to Mother? Even on *good* days, her conditioned reflexes have her sitting on the edge of her chair—anything can happen.

A friend told me that sometimes when her kids are playing at someone else's house, even as old as they are now (eight and six), she can't relax for very long. Not hearing them about, not being reassured that they aren't getting into some trouble always leaves her slightly uncomfortable.

"Oh," you say, "she must be a lunatic." But years of worrying about children and feeling guilt and fear from the start accumulate, becoming a habit. And unlike most bad habits, it can't be broken because it has pure love as its foundation. A woman who does not care about her children does not feel these things. And, it could easily be said, vice versa.

"Oh, but what are a few accidents now and again? That's life." True. So are illnesses. And, when one is effusively describing the joys of parenthood these things are rarely mentioned.

Did you know that a young child can run a fever even when there is no infection? And a high fever frequently can be more dangerous than the illness, if any. Every mother I know has labored, at least once, to get a child's temperature down, sometimes without knowing what caused it, because a high fever can cause convulsions.

One mother found it out when it happened to her six-month-old baby boy. She had taken him to the doctor, given him his medication, and he seemed to be getting better. She put him down for the night, comforted that he was improving. A short time later when she looked in on him, she found him in the middle of a convulsion.

Although parents become fairly "seasoned," the anxiety is always there. One young woman insists that mothers with especially healthy children suffer even more when their kids are actually sick: "They're sick so seldom," she says of her two children. "that even a mild cold or temperature terrifies me. I always worry about brain damage." In describing how she reacts, she said, "I'm useless. I'm no good in a crisis when the kids are sick—I just can't handle it." Added to the worry, there is always the nagging feeling that a better mother would have prevented this particular illness somehow.

One couple I talked to admitted taking shifts for one week because their three-month-old baby had a slight cold. They were too frightened to leave him unattended. Night after night they took turns sitting up in a chair in the baby's room.

Incidentally, for those who might believe that breast-fed babies are immune to colds, flu, and other illnesses, it's interesting that three other mothers who nursed their babies said that when their children got sick for the first time, they were still nursing them. (To lay another old wives' tale to rest, my doctor's warning that breast-feeding is by no means a sure-fire contraceptive device has been borne out by two very unhappy, very pregnant, very breast-feeding friends.)

The way mothers react to their children's illnesses can be summed up in the words of one pediatrician when he said, "In most cases mothers wind up being sicker than their children just from their own anxiety."

And children are not the only members of the family to get sick. Someone once said that mothers are unusually healthy because there's no percentage in being sick, at least not until their kids are teenagers. If her illness is severe enough, a mother can get someone to help out. But usually it's just a bad cold or a simple little 101° fever that doesn't quite justify paying money to a sitter. There are no sick days for mothers or, as one of them said after recovering from a bout with the flu, "What was I supposed to do—walk into my baby's room in the morning and tell him I was sorry that I was sick and wouldn't be coming in to work today?"

I have a friend—a kind and patient woman—who painfully and skillfully raised two now-grown children. Looking back, she lamented that "if only I could have afforded a little help, it would have been easier—I could have been a better and happier mother. No one ever helped *me*."

When I mentioned to her one day that a friend was agonizing over a serious problem with her two oldest children, she snapped back, "Well, she has money; she can afford all the help she needs." When another friend was suffering from a physical illness caused by nervous tension, she was unrelenting: "What's she got to be so nervous about? She's got money and only one child, and all the nice clothes anyone could want."

It is perfectly true—and it would be foolish to deny —that many women have gotten immense relief from having help. One friend of mine works at a job that she doesn't even particularly like, saying, "If I didn't have help and if I hadn't had it all during these years, I have absolutely no doubt that they would have put me away long ago." Many women employ help, especially when their children are young, not so much to help with the chores as to enable them to maintain an illusion of freedom, a feeling that they are not responsible for *every* need of their children.

Being able to afford a housekeeper and a baby nurse, nice clothes, and vacations doesn't let a mother off the hook. "The buck stops here" is as true for a mother as it was for Harry Truman. Take the kids out of homemaking, for example, and the tasks are a snap, but take the homemaking out of the responsibility associated with caring for kids, and you're still left with an enormous and tension-filled job. The straightforward general maintenance is not all that time-consuming. Ask any working girl how much time it takes her to keep things up, and ask any childless couple who share the chores what is involved.

The buck that stops here is the one that no housekeeper or baby nurse can take for Mom. When your child is doing poorly in school, no amount of floors waxed for you is any comfort. It just means that you don't have to scrub the floor while you are worrying. When your child is running a temperature of 104°, it doesn't matter one bit that you can afford to take off for a weekend trip or go on a vacation. When your child has just been brought home by the police, unless you are irretrievably superficial, looking at a healthy checking account balance is not where it's at.

No maid or housekeeper can relieve you of the ultimate responsibility of guiding your child or relieve you of worrying about your child. No hired help can always be there to get up in the middle of the night, go over to the school when there's a problem, take your child to the dentist, doctor, Scout meetings, Brownies, and attend the PTA meeting for you.

No one who scrubs her own floor, is dying for a day out of the house—or is just exhausted—is asked to feel sorry for someone who has trouble with the servants. I do suggest, however, that anyone who feels that pain-free parenthood is insured simply because she can afford to pay someone to take care of the drudgery had better think again. She'd better know, just for openers, that the domestic labor force is a declining one.

A woman with help sums it up nicely: "In the final analysis, no one but you can raise your child or children the way you feel is proper. No one but the parents can possibly feel the pain associated with the doubt, fear, and guilt of that responsibility. Whether it be a question of toilet-training or your choice of spiritual guidance, having a housekeeper and nurse, say, may relieve you of some of the drudgery, but ultimately the parents are responsible for the orientation and happiness of the children and their impact on society. And that's a very heavy trip."

5

Hi, I'm Mommy.
fly me to the
cuckoo's nest

WHILE I'M SITTING HERE writing, there are four kids playing in another room. If I recorded the audio accompanying their "playing Scrabble" (that's what they tell me they are doing) there would be shrieks, thumps, crashes, chatter, doors slamming, the sloshing of liquids, and occasional laughter, and constantly. Not a single second contains only the sound of the typewriter. And today is a good day because they remembered to turn off the television set when they quit watching. It will soon grow very quiet, however, and that is the signal that they have now begun to misbehave seriously.

But for now, all of this racket is setting the stage for this mother to have a real case of nerves by about five o'clock. The racket is stacked up next to the three fights that I broke up within the last half hour, jumping up and down every two minutes to answer the phone or the door, or to get the dog back into the yard so she doesn't get pregnant or hit by a car, the numerous requests for food, water, juice, Coke, and chewing gum in between the breakfast routine, the lunch routine, and my daily janitorial chores. I'm now starting to view another day slipping by —another day when success or failure will be measured by how depressed or nauseated I will be once we somehow get through it. Another day that I will set against all of the others, nearly identical—with the knowledge that tomorrow will be the same.

Many women are able to cope with the joys of motherhood. Many are not. For the woman who finds it extremely difficult, the result can be a life of horror and self-hatred. For my friend Jean it became a life of horror; her lengthy discussion of how she felt could be the story of many mothers.

The first time I noticed I no longer had "nerves of steel" came while I was calmly sipping a cup of coffee in a friend's kitchen. I had taken my children, two and three years old, to play with my friend's little four-year-old boy. It has been a nerve-wracking drive on the freeway, but I managed it neatly—or so I thought. In any case, while Linda and I sat talking, her doorbell suddenly rang and I understood the expression "I jumped out of my skin." I did just that.

I was rather surprised. But because I have a long history of keeping cool during confusion and clamor and being able to work calmly under pressure, I attributed it to the freeway with the kids, maybe that second cup of coffee, or a combination of the two. I didn't recognize it as the first signal that I was gradually becoming jumpy and tense—the first step toward deep depression. The roots of all of this can probably be traced back to the very beginning—the day I first felt anxiety about a new baby, and the rush of conflicting emotions and fears that apparently all new mothers have. From that point, I just started building my negative bank account, while I still appeared to be fairly calm for a few years.

To illustrate how the geometric progression took hold, and how quickly it can work, I can recall a friend saying to me, during the midst of a batch of kids generating noise and confusion, "Jean, I don't see how you can stand it. You're so *calm*." I also remember commenting sincerely that it really didn't bother me. But just a few months later, the jangling of the telephone could set my nerves on edge, the sound of something dropping could make my skin crawl, and more and more I was feeling that sudden twinge in the pit of my stomach over very trivial incidents.

Now, four years later, I can hardly be described as calm or serene, and it is doubtful that I ever will be.

The best that can be said is that I make a valiant and successful effort to maintain control; I've learned many tricks to keep my head and body in good shape, but the trip has been an arduous one, punctuated with very dark days when I feared I was losing my grip entirely, or would become physically very seriously ill.

While I mistakenly assumed that I was adjusting to child-generated confusion and noise, I was instead becoming sensitized to it, a fact that made itself known for the first time the day I reacted so strongly to the sound of a doorbell. The truth is I was becoming sensitized in a number of different but interlocking ways. The real difficulty comes in recognizing that something is happening and then knowing what to do about it. For me, this was very difficult since I've always enjoyed good health and an overall sense of well-being.

So, one day came that held the answer to my new jumpiness and nervousness. That was the first time I noticed tingling sensations in my legs and arms, quickly followed by numbness. I wasn't at all relieved at my assessment of the situation and I made an appointment to see a doctor, fully convinced that I was very seriously ill. I seemed to have the symptoms of Parkinson's disease. I also considered that I might have a brain tumor or a grave neurological disorder. After the doctor examined me briefly, we returned to his office and I expressed my fears.

He laughed. Then he gave his diagnosis: "Nerves." *Nerves!* Since when do nerves cause all of these physical conditions? I could understand the upset stomach and headache, but some of the other symptoms seemed almost like seizures. And besides I'd always been quite calm. Surely something else, something physical, was at work. I'd always believed that even under great stress people could talk themselves into semi-tranquillity at least—by just refusing to give in.

At least partly convinced that the diagnosis was correct, I accepted the doctor's prescription for tranquilizers, but firmly resolved not to use them unless I couldn't function otherwise. A couple of years back, a friend of mine told me that she'd learned how to cope with her maternal responsibilities—as she produced a bottle of innocent-looking white tablets from her purse, saying simply, "Equanil." I recall my reaction —I thought she was weak.

For better or worse, I kept my promise to myself by not taking the medication as it had been prescribed; instead I took a pill only when my physical symptoms got in the way of taking care of my responsibilities. Generally, I'd cope with a few dizzy spells, some visual problems, and continually sweating palms and feet; but when I drove the car, I recognized that it was only responsible to take something that restored my coordination. I found out later that driving on tranquilizers can be dangerous. I was so afraid of getting hooked on these hated tranquilizers that I actually damaged my physical health by allowing all that adrenaline to course through my body constantly; at the same time, I underwent another milestone of sorts. I felt incredibly guilty about having to take tranquilizers to perform even simple tasks, like driving, and at the same time I was living with the gnawing fear that the situation could get even worse. That fear was reinforced on one lovely Saturday afternoon last summer when I nearly lost consciousness. I was convinced I was having a heart attack. I became weak, my heart was pounding, and I broke out into a cold sweat. Too weak to do anything else, I simply went to bed, resolving that as soon as I could muster the strength, I'd call my sister or a friend so that there would be someone on hand to look after the kids who were luckily at the home of a playmate. Fortunately, I'd done the right thing at the right time and within a half hour I felt better.

Like Jean, I've taken tranquilizers, but always with the feeling that it was still another piece of evidence that I was a very imperfect mother. I've learned that I'm *far* from being alone.

Melissa, an affluent, well-groomed, seemingly serene forty-year-old mother of three teenagers, has pursued a career although there was never a financial need. I learned what motivated her. She said that when the children were

95

still fairly young, she developed what appeared to be a heart condition. Her physician told her flatly that there was nothing wrong with her heart, or physically with her at all for that matter, but if she didn't get herself out of the house and away from the kids, she'd be in very serious trouble. She had displayed all of the same symptoms Jean had and a few more. It was difficult to believe that this confident, intelligent woman had been reduced to the level she was describing. But by now her two oldest children were away at college and she had only one fifteen-year-old boy at home. She fully enjoyed her work and, while she had felt guilty about what she termed her "unsuitability for motherhood" in the past, she had come to terms with it many years before. As she put it, "I felt guilty about pursuing a career and leaving the kids with sitters, and it was very difficult to bear the responsibilities of a home and family while working full time; but had I not, the kids might not have any mother at all."

Vicki is another mother who never left home.

It finally got so bad that one day I just passed out. I'd been taking tranquilizers for years and hating it. I gradually was attempting to make it on my own with my ultimate goal being to quit relying on medication. I realize now that I picked a lousy time to try. We had holiday house guests, the kids were on their Christmas vacation, and it was pretty hectic. Anyway, one day I just started hyperventilating [breathing very hard] like mad, and then I was out like a light. The next day I did two things: I took a tranquilizer when I first got up, and I made an appointment to see a psychiatrist.

It took only one visit with the psychiatrist to fully understand the level of my problem, and what needed to be done. I continued with sedation, and I learned to force myself to relax to the extent that when it really got bad, I'd just say, "The hell with it." That may sound simple. It isn't. Oh, yes, I also reinforced my entire program with vitamin therapy and plenty of rest. Things are a lot better now, but of course, one of the kids is in college and the two others have become fairly independent and I can see the light at the end of the tunnel, and know that in about five more years, I'll be fairly free from the picky details of raising kids.

Another mother of four planned children is Dina. She readily admits that if she had it to do over again, knowing what the realities are involved in coping with four youngsters, she would not have *any* children. In discussing her two-year bout with severe anxiety, she said it all converged in one day:

Oh, nothing really special happened. But suddenly I just had to get away. I walked into our bedroom and locked the door, walked into our bathroom and locked the door, then went into the shower, closing the door behind me, and sat on the floor for a very long time—doing nothing—just sitting. I was coming apart at the seams. You know, I always thought I was fairly stable, but when the children were small, my hands would shake. I would have fits of depression, cry for no apparent reason. I finally went to see a psychiatrist. It helped.

Dina is the picture of calm repose and is magnificent with her children. Dina feels that what ultimately saved her from a complete breakdown was getting a job outside the home. She didn't need the money; she needed the salvation. Oddly enough she is thriving, although the job is tension-filled and the environment highly competitive. It is, however, she notes, very different from the tension of being a housewife and mother, and far easier to cope with. But she feels, guiltily, that she is a rotten mother, and she has a constant fear that the tensions of yesterday will return someday without warning.

I've known few mothers who haven't suffered from tension, depression, or emotionally induced trauma in varying degrees. Nearly all the mothers I've talked to rely on something external to help them cope with the difficulties of raising children. For some it's alcohol, for others it is tranquilizers, and others use food. Many women who work confess that they work to help relieve their anxiety—although they suffer frequently from large doses of guilt.

Sociologist Jesse Bernard, in noting in a recent interview that far more housewives are likely to suffer insomnia, depressions, and nervous breakdowns than working women, feels that housework ". . . may have a deteriorating effect upon her mind, rendering her incapable of prolonged concentration on any single task." Further, she does her tedious job in isolation—unlike her predecessors, who shared tougher manual chores with members of an extended family:

Far fewer than expected of the working women and more than expected of the housewives, for example, had actually had a nervous breakdown. Fewer than expected of the working women and more than expected of the housewives suffered from nervousness, inertia, insomnia, trembling hands, nightmares, perspiring hands, fainting, headaches, dizziness and heart palpitations. The housewife syndrome is far from a figment of anyone's imagination . . . in terms of the number of people involved, the housewife syndrome might well be viewed as public health problem number one.

6

School days

PART OF THE REASON we live where we do is that the public school system here is among the finest in the state of California, if not in the entire nation. As any mother would be, I'm grateful that my children are receiving the benefits of first-rate schools and magnificent teaching. And so I hope my comments will show only one parent's reaction to the demands and special problems of having kids in school anywhere and will in no way reflect upon the fine teachers my children presently have and justifiably adore.

"Just wait until the kids are in school" is something struggling mothers of toddlers hear. The rest of the sentence is conveniently omitted somehow. Whatever respite is provided by having the public school system babysit for several hours, and however great the school system may be, it's all balanced by still another dimension of parenthood we novice-mothers are ill-prepared for.

For a mother who has been taking care of pre-schoolers at home without help, there is certainly no question that, when the children are in school, her hours will be shorter. Not that much shorter in many cases where schools are on half-session through high school, but shorter. The fantasy of many mothers—that when their children go off to school they will live a life of freedom and leisure—is only partly true. (Many mothers who assumed they would march off blithely to work when their children were in school found themselves shocked to realize that children get sick, schools declare vacations, and there is, of course, the good old summertime.) First, a larger than imagined number of time-consuming school-related activities impinge on that leisure time. Second, the demands generated by having children in school are frequently not only time-consuming, but emotion-consuming.

A child's life may not be warped if you change a diaper less often than you ought to, but as the child grows the acts you perform with him and for him seem to take on a greater urgency. You are concerned that he may be affected badly and for all time if you do not pay close attention to his schooling. It is hard enough to meet his emotional needs, but the assumption of most parents is that the school will see to the education, at least, of the child. All too often that assumption proves unwarranted.

One New York mother told me that in California we have it all. True, ours is a free system, and at its best our free system is as good as any private one in the nation. Yet the schools in many areas have become a disgrace, although homeowners pay premium amounts in taxes; even the best system in the state is wanting because, periodically, there are bad teachers. The mother of three boys, herself an elementary school teacher said, "To assume because our school system is one of the best that each and every teacher is first-rate is a mistake. You get bad teachers in good systems and good teachers in bad systems."

But most parents don't indulge in statistical analyses of school systems. Most of us are concerned with how our children are doing, how we are doing, about our children's inadequacies, and about our inadequacies as parents. Many mothers have complained that their kids can speak Spanish or French, but don't know how to read English. Two college instructors have told me that a growing number of their students, although bright, are "functional illiterates."

Parents complain in increasing numbers that the schools are attempting to mold the morals of their children, and that the parents, unskilled to the task, are having to teach the basics.

When I sent Lisa off to school for the first time, she

101

had one year of nursery school under her belt (to prepare her for kindergarten—today, nearly a requirement). The only other preparation I had for this phase of her life (and a year later for Adam's) was that *I* had gone to school. Drawing from my own experience, I assumed my children would, in their early years, learn the same things I had—the basic tools. The matter of my morals, sociability, chess, music lessons, or philately were pretty much left up to me and my parents. The matter of teaching me how to read and write was left up to those whose training and skills were equal to the task—the teachers.

There are approximately two dozen kids in our neighborhood who attend the same school. There were, a year ago, two teachers teaching first grade. I will call them for the sake of this discussion Mrs. A and Mrs. B. Those who went to Mrs. A's class learned to read; those who went to Mrs. B's class learned to read with home assistance, or with special outside reading classes, or simply didn't learn. As one seven-year-old girl said, "My brother had Mrs. B. and she didn't teach. I'm sure glad I got Mrs. A."

Lisa was in Mrs. B's class. I tutored her every night, but I'm not a gifted teacher (that's why I didn't choose it as a profession), and my help to her was, at best, dubious. The next step for her is a remedial reading class—unheard of for an average or bright student in my day.

One of the areas where I honestly feel that I fail my kids is in helping them with their homework. And, more and more, I'm finding that once the children are in school, so is Mother once again. Every night one hour of my time is set aside for helping them with reading, math, spelling, and other lessons. We try to adhere to a specific time each evening to ensure that the homework doesn't get neglected. Now that I've gotten into a routine of helping them, I really don't mind too much. For one as ill-equipped as I in the teaching of young children, this is slightly more than a challenge, but I've yet to meet the parent who embraces such tutoring with welcome arms.

An informal poll I conducted revealed that most of the mothers had no idea that they would be required to help their children with homework, and had in fact never given it a thought until it was presented to them as part of their maternal responsibilities. Most of those who indicated that they were fairly conscientious about helping the kids with their studies conveyed an attitude of resigned reluctance. Many mothers just somehow never got around to it, and one or two did all of the homework themselves. A few others said they felt it was the school's job to educate their children.

One mother said that she doesn't help her kids because she doesn't understand the work, and the kids think she's stupid so they don't even ask for her help (stupid like a fox). Still another said she doesn't help because there are four kids and it's just too much—in fact, she went on to say, it's too much even if she and her husband divide them up. Another, echoing many, told me she helps but, "it's a real drag and I resent it."

The issue of homework is one that points up a major difficulty for many mothers in raising children. I would be less than candid if I said that I did not resent having to help my children with homework. It is not enjoyable time, and I resent the school for forcing me to spend time in a way that I find unpleasant. But more important than the time is the pressure on me not to fail my children, to make certain that I am doing all that I can to help them to grow up well. Similarly I resent the time it takes to involve myself in school activities. But most important is my feeling that my concern for my children's well-being is constantly being measured by the degree to which I participate.

It is no criticism of our school system, nor is it a reflection of my love for our children, that I do not like to bake cookies for carnivals, deliver cookies, serve as a Room Mother, attend school board meetings, go to open house, or run telephone trees (a latter-day version of Indian smoke signals in which mothers convey vital school messages to other mothers). I can't volunteer for a car pool, because, fortunately, I have no car; the PTA is a drag; and parent-teacher conferences scare me. In fact, participating to the limited extent I do is torture, and I can honestly say that there are no other people in the world for whom I would make such supreme sacrifices.

But I do feel incredibly guilty when I either choose to or have to say a firm "no" to a teacher when she asks me to participate in some program involving the kids. On one occasion Adam volunteered me to serve as a monitor for a field trip (without first asking me about it), and I simply could not do it. Some friends of ours were moving here from the East; they were driving, but the movers were expected on that particular day, and they were to call me when they got here. I might have to supervise the moving and placement of the furniture—I couldn't very well say to these people who were counting on us: "Gee, I don't know what happened, because I went on a field trip." I know that the teacher shared my opinion that I was being a real dud of a mother, but what was more important was my son's disappointment.

The telephone tree, a project for which I've said a firm "no" more than once, is generally used to galvanize us errant parents into action. But most school functions are announced in advance by little notices that little people bring home to big people who don't look at them because they get so many of these little pieces of paper that they get lost in the accumulation of other papers, bills, grocery lists, appointment reminders, and all the clutter that makes up Mom's desk (or space on the drainboard, actually). As one mother of four put it, "What really overwhelms me about raising children is all those goddam notes and little pieces of paper they bring home from school." Some of these things are veritable pamphlets, but most of them are precise little reminders that ask you to *do* something. And when the school asks you to do *anything,* you feel you must. I have a two-inch-thick folder of these tiny consciences on little pieces of paper—representing only one school year's worth.

Once, when I was working and Lisa was in kindergarten, I received a call at the office from her school. I got the usual symptoms of, "My God, something terrible has happened"; the call, however, was to inquire if I had received a notice inviting me to a mother-daughter fashion

104

show. I resisted the temptation to tell her that the notice must be sitting next to an invitation for the Mad Hatter's Tea Party because I hadn't seen it, and instead said, "I haven't seen the notice." I explained (guiltily) that I worked full time and couldn't come. The teacher (who must have known that, because she called me at my office) was most convincing when she expressed her sincere disappointment that I would not be joining them in this and other, similar, functions. I think I got my first inkling then of how primary school teachers (whether they themselves are mothers or not) disapprove of working mothers. The teacher's disappointment, however, was no match for my daughter's. I felt a little guilty when I talked to the teacher, but it really hit home when Lisa let me know how she felt. I promised her that I would participate in the next school function, no matter what.

The next function to come along was a tea for the mothers at the nursery school—Adam's school. The little kids had baked nut bread for the occasion, and Adam was terribly excited about the event. So I went, with Lisa feeling really out of sorts as she said, "You go to Adam's school, but *never* to mine."

Even a fairly conscientious mother finds it difficult to believe that she is doing enough if she cannot attend every school function. After missing one or two, the teacher's cordial, "Glad to see you, Mrs. X; we missed you last time," brings home the guilt.

A good example of what I mean is open house at the school, which takes place about two or four times per child each year. You usually find out about open house when you have just settled into a chair, clutching a drink, vowing that you would not leave the house for a million dollars because you have just had one of the rottenest days of the year. Then, in they come: *"Open house tonight, Mama."* Your husband looks at you with utter dread, proclaiming that he won't budge—he's out on his feet, and *he* has just had one of the rottenest days of the year. In the end, you both go to open house because you cannot bear seeing your child being hurt over your apparent lack of interest—and "Mommy, I've made special drawings and cleaned out my desk just for your visit."

I have often wondered if other parents feel as ridiculous and out of place as we two admitted misfits do. It's a very phony scene—you look at snakes, white rabbits, white rats, kids' drawings, and neat (and sometimes messy) desks, and you sense that everyone is slightly uncomfortable. If you are uninterested and forcing enthusiasm, you feel a bit guilty, even if your deception is successful. And if your interest isn't genuine, as every good parent's should be, you feel distinctly lacking.

There are many time-consuming things that happen once the kids are in school that have less to do with their being in school than with their being of school age. Next year, for example, Adam will be in the Cub Scouts, and this year Lisa will be in the Brownies. Already, I've heard a rumor that the mothers of Brownies are expected to participate fully—otherwise the children can't join. So, unless I become part of the organization, I will deprive my daughter of something she wants very much. When I was in Brownies, my mother's participation consisted of buying me a uniform.

The mothers I know whose children have been through the age where scouting of some sort is in order say almost in unison, "I participated, and it was torture." There was a lot of work, a large commitment of time, and more important, the obligation to do specific things at specific times added to an already full schedule of child guidance and family obligations. Those mothers who served have said that they were pressured into it by a combination of guilt feelings and their children's comments like, "Jennie's mother *likes* to do these things—why can't you be more like Jennie's mother?"

Parents strong enough to withstand the pressure to get them to serve as leaders can't escape the "homework" that goes with children's extra-currricular activities—another inevitable and unanticipated aspect of parenthood that becomes gradually accepted as part of child-rearing. As one mother put it: "In addition to having to help the kids with their school work, my son's Scoutmaster called me the other night and asked me if I couldn't please help the boy with his knots." This lady knows from *naught* about knots, so how can she help? By learning about knots first, which she will do, of course, to avoid feeling guilty. "It's not that that one specific thing is a lot to ask. It's that I have four children, a husband, and a dog. All of them have needs, and I can ignore the dog, but not the rest. Every single special extra from homework to knots can add up to many hours each week, until I have a long list of things to do, all trivial, that hangs over my head—the knots, the PTA meeting, the cookies for the carnival all become part of one heavy burden."

Another mother who has one son had this to say: "No sooner had we finished with Cub Scouts—I was a den mother—than, the next thing I knew we were deeply involved with Little League." And another, Susan, the mother of three lovely daughters, felt that parenthood was lovely and easy before her kids were in school—before they reached that special age when they have social activities. Now she finds that she must run over to the school at least once a day to deliver a forgotten lunch or misplaced homework or raincoats; she spends the rest of the time that the girls are in school running errands, cleaning house, and keeping up with the family's laundry. "Making sure that dinner preparations are well under way before school is out is imperative, because I spend the afternoon carting the kids to and from their various music lessons and scouting activities, to the library, the doctor, the dentist, the orthodontist, and the variety store to pick up binders, paper, pencils, or whatever tools they need desperately for their school work."

Rhoda, the mother of two girls, described it this way:

The big problem I had is that they wanted mothers or fathers to come in twice a quarter—eight times a year per child. With the first child I couldn't go because I was working and it was like, well, I was sending her to school to get her away from me, so she could get out in the world alone. Besides, I had enough of kids at home. Since I worked I got out of it by promising to make some smocks for the kids; the teacher said the school would supply the material. After I said, "sure," they never asked me again nor did they bring me the material. Even the smocks, or the promise of them, didn't keep me from feeling guilty, though, because my daughter wanted me to come and all the other mothers went. Even if *all* of them don't go to everything, the kids whose mothers don't go to a particular function always feel that everyone else's mother came. The guilt is there because if every other mother is doing it and your child wants you to be there, you feel it. If no one else did it then there wouldn't be any guilt feelings.

My mother used to go to PTA meetings, and she helped out at things, but I don't remember asking her to, and lots of other mothers in my child's school have the same memory. I think this sort of thing with the schools is a kind of reinforcement that we are a child-oriented society. But this thing—this *fad*—could be bad, because we might have children more dependent on their parents. The whole idea of going to school is not just to learn, but to get away from Mommy, now isn't it?

Audrey echoed Rhoda: "I'd like to know who came up with the idea that we need to coordinate the parents with the school and the school with the child, and so on. It must be considered to be better that a child have a 'medium' environment than have all school or all parents. I never had my mother in *my* kindergarten. I never had my mother all the way through elementary school—the teachers didn't want the parents there. It's a new trend. To me all of this interacting with the schools hasn't been all that beneficial. When the kids get in first grade, as long as you ask your child what he is reading, you can find out directly from your child. If I feel guilty for not doing some of the things, imagine how mothers who work—who have to work—feel when they can't participate."

It's easy to say that these mothers are simply rationalizing away their desire to have their children in school and, by definition, away from them. The reaction of many people is to say how selfish mothers are who want time for themselves and who, admittedly, would like to have their children out of the way for at least some of the time. (Many women who have been unable to work before their children were in school find it easier to do so afterward, making the logical assumption that as long as the children are *supposed* not to be with them, then it's okay to be away from them.) Are mothers selfish to want the school to take the children off their hands for a while? Perhaps. But presumably the children do have to get an education, do have to mix with other children in order to grow up. It seems unfair to be too harsh on women who resent the fact that, what for many of them is their only guilt-free time away from the children (the kids are *supposed* to be in school, so it's okay) is impinged on. Is the only acceptable definition of a good mother a mother who wishes with all her heart to be with her children at all times?

Now that I'm no longer working away from home, I try to go to most functions because it is important to the kids. But what about the mothers who can't go to anything—how do they feel? How do their kids feel? Sometimes a mother is ill, or she may have another child sick at home; sometimes she may be a working mother. If she is particularly interested, she is disappointed, and to her own disappointment she must add that of her child. It is easy for her to feel that she is the only mother who is guilty of letting her child down.

The *time* taken by school-related activities pales next to the *toll* they take on many women. Spending time at school is not merely baking cookies and tying knots. It is learning precisely how much is demanded of you, of being judged, and of having others evaluate you, your children, and your ability as a mother.

One young woman, who sadly is probably not much of an exception, found herself caught in a vicious trap. She was a working mother who, while she enjoyed her job, worked for the money. Her husband had become ill and could not support the family, so she worked to put the food on the table and pay the rent. For many reasons, she did not feel she was a very good mother, but having to take a job and leave the family home each day only added to her already poor self-image. Because of her job she could not attend most of the school functions, or participate in the PTA, and sometimes she found it difficult to attend even the all-important parent-teacher conferences. When she finally worked it out with her employer so that she had time to attend one or two events at the school, she found, after a few attempts, that she still couldn't do it. Couldn't because she was frightened. By this time she had missed so many functions, even important meetings with the teacher, that she felt she was truly a bad mother; she was convinced that her son's teacher thought so too, and that the other parents viewed her with disapproval. She went to a few programs, and with each one she became progressively more nervous and self-conscious, feeling more and more out of step with what was going on. On those occasions when she made a monumental effort to go to a conference, tea, or PTA meeting, she would feel frightened and inadequate. Having the teacher say, "Glad to see you; we missed you last time" was not received in the spirit it was intended, but instead was taken as a criticism of her failure to be more active.

The last function this mother attended was a parent-teacher conference to review her son's progress and his problems. This already frightened and self-conscious woman literally dragged herself over to the school for an anticipated ordeal to find the teacher obviously distressed over this "problem child." Instead of beginning with a review of the child's academic progress, or discussing his strong and weak points in specific subjects, the teacher marched over to his desk and flung it open. "Look at this. It's a mess." According to the mother, it was indeed that, with papers and books and pieces of pencils and all sorts of garbage stirred up together. The mother nodded, while the teacher went on, "And he doesn't sit still during class. He chews pencils, and then he breaks them up into little tiny pieces, and really, Mrs. L., it is driving me out of my mind." The boy's mother was too nervous to do more than

110

mutter, "I know." The teacher's polemic became even more furious as she ticked off all the child's bad qualities (he didn't seem to have any good ones), and finally she said, "Mrs. L., this boy is incorrigible. You must take him to a psychiatrist." Mrs. L. said simply, "Why?" At this the teacher just screamed, "WHY???"

Mrs. L. fled, terrified, and that was the last time she ever set foot into anything resembling the Mt. View-Los Altos Unified School District. It was less painful to be a guilty, brooding failure.

This mother knew better than anyone that the boy was rapidly becoming a problem, and she feels that the teacher behaved in a completely understandable manner under the circumstances. She blames herself and her circumstances for all of her son's problems.

Perhaps Mrs. L. is right about her shortcomings and perhaps not. But it is a fact that the teachers of our children do indeed scare the hell out of most of us. They look us over, they judge us, and often, when they aren't judging us, we feel that they are. Yet, we believe they possess extraordinary expertise in judging our children's morals, manners, and psyches, and we sometimes mistakenly look to them for all the answers.

Way back when their children are infants, mothers have a way of comparing notes in a competitive fashion. It may start when little Freddie can hold his head up first, or little Jenny cuts the first tooth, or little Stevie becomes potty-trained before the rest of his contemporaries. But certainly it is seen more completely when the kids are in school. We mothers then start comparing notes on when the kids read, how much the teachers like our kids, and, in those schools where grading is still in force, on grades.

One mother commented obliquely on that aspect of having children in school:

I suppose I was as concerned as anyone else with whether or not my children walked or talked early or late, but it wasn't until I got them into school that I began to see the real complications and competition.

111

Actually, it began even before my daughter entered school. We live in New York where neighborhood public schools are so bad that private schools are almost a necessity. But I wasn't prepared for the competitiveness. For the upper middle class in New York, having one's child in the "right" school is ten times more important than having gone to the "right" college oneself. Practically the first question one is asked on meeting new people is: "Where do your children go to school?"

It becomes a status symbol and parents practically prostitute themselves to get their children in—partly for themselves and partly because they've been brainwashed or have brainwashed themselves into believing that the status schools give their kids a better education. Perhaps they do, but one wonders. Can you imagine looking at your two-and-a-half-year-old (one generally starts nursery school in New York at three and applies a year ahead of time) and wondering whether to curse yourself for not being charming enough at your interview or your child for not being charming at his? Once you're in, of course, even putting aside the pressure to dress your child like the other children and make yourself look like the other mommies, the inevitable comparisons and fears begin. Is he as bright as the rest? Why is he so active compared to Jeff and Richard? Why doesn't he share better? Am I doing something wrong? The self-doubt about whether you're doing it right grows with every comparison.

Joseph and Lois Bird write in *Power to the Parents:*

A parent-teacher conference or welcoming talk at the school open house takes on the flavor of shop talk at a psychology convention—if psychologists talked in nothing but clichés. ("I am happy to say, Mrs. Smith, that Johnny seems to adjust well to competitive situations and is able to establish comfortable relationships with his peers, although he does seem somewhat insecure when called upon to assert his individuality and natural creativity.") Teachers who face thirty children in a classroom—and have no more experience or training in diagnosing and treating psychological problems than the school custodian—"authoritatively" analyze young Jimmy who has been sitting in the sixth seat, third row, for five weeks. They then advise Jimmy's parents. Of course, Jimmy's parents have been living with Jimmy for nine years, but the teacher "by reason of her training" is better able in five weeks to psych out thirty kids than their parents are. Of course, if the teacher is a bit insecure in her diagnosis, or if Jimmy is a problem in the classroom she feels she can't handle, she can send him to the counselor. The counselor or school psychologist can then approach Jimmy's poor academic performance or misbehavior on the playground as a neurosis. There is a very real fear on the part of many parents that they will do the "wrong" thing, i.e., psychologically damaging, if they take action on their own without first seeking the advice of the teacher or if they ignore the teacher's advice.[1]

It is our confusion, I think, that makes us so ready to pin the label of "expert" on anyone who works with children, or seems to know more about guiding them than we do. If we are having problems with our kids, that seems to be enough reason to believe that we don't know what we are doing.

Like many mothers, I feel inadequate to the task of disciplining and instilling values, and so I find myself giving great weight to every word the children's teachers utter. I have found myself asking for advice from a divorced woman who has never had children of her own. And then feeling guilty when she implied I didn't spend time with my child, didn't provide enough enriching experiences, didn't help enough with the lessons.

I have talked to many mothers who would do virtually anything the teacher recommended, from simple help with their children's lessons, to seeking psychiatric treatment or drug therapy to calm down their "hyperactive" youngsters.

As one mother put it, "My son's teacher, who took a psych course in college, is younger than I and has no children. Yet she explained how sibling rivalry, my husband's indifference to school activities, and the part-time job I

113

held last year were causing my child deep emotional disturbances that were interfering with his ability to learn. At the time, I hung on her every word. Looking back, I realize that in an effort to do the right thing I was grasping at straws."

"Whenever I talk to my daughter's teacher," said Kay, "I come away from the meeting first feeling inadequate, of course, for not helping her more with her school work, being a disaster as a tutor, and not spending more time with her. But more than that, I leave with an impression that the teacher thinks I have no responsibilities except for Lucy. That I don't have a husband with needs, another child with needs, a house to clean, or an obligation to myself. That the time Lucy is in school is just free time that enables me to devote my life to my daughter when she's not in school."

For the elementary grades in our district, parent-teacher conferences have replaced report cards, so there are an unusual number of them. The regular ones take place four times each school year, and then there are the other conferences that are called for special problems. (Most mothers average at least two of these per child per year—a "special problem" is whatever the teacher decides it is.)

I prepare for these meetings as if I either were going to play Lady Macbeth to an audience of thousands or go into court to face murder charges.

To an already anxious mother, any problem her child has is magnified out of all proportion, and each conference, each unpleasant or worrisome session, provides more negative information to add to the store. Here are some excerpts from one of my remembered sessions.

TEACHER: Let's first discuss her physical disabilities.
MOTHER: Physical disabilities?
TEACHER: Yes. They're quite severe, and you don't seem to be doing anything about these problems. What, for example, have you done about her *hearing?*
MOTHER: I explained all that to the school nurse. She has allergies, and when they're raging it affects her hearing

114

as well as her respiratory system. I give her a decongestant three times each day, and——

TEACHER: Well, she talks too much and too loudly.

MOTHER (incredulous): LISA? Talks too much and too loudly? Why, on my last visit I was told that she was shy, quiet, and didn't participate in class.

TEACHER: Well, she talks too loudly and I can't do anything with her. When it occurs, I bring her up in front of the class and make her sit on the floor so that perhaps she can be shamed into better behavior—encouraged by having the other children looking at her.

MOTHER: (Speechless)

TEACHER: And what about her vision? Haven't you gotten her glasses yet? It's been quite some time since we advised you of her problem.

MOTHER (muttering): We were on our way to get them today.

TEACHER: Good. When do you think they'll be ready? (sighing) Frankly, Mrs. Radl, try as I may, I really can't find any strong points in Lisa.

MOTHER: Oh.

TEACHER: And the thumb-sucking. It's gotten so much worse. Since I started teaching this class in January she's gotten worse every day. And she gets her papers wet with her thumbs, and when I speak to her about this, and her other, ah, problems, she starts sucking her hair. . . . She needs a good deal of help. . . . Perhaps, a surrogate mother`. . . ah . . . to help her over the rough spots . . .

I took my clammy hands and feet, throbbing head, and water-filled eyes away from that meeting just as fast as I could. My failure as a mother was obviously crippling my child intellectually and emotionally for life. My friend who had kindly driven me to the school turned to me and said, "Shirl, I've never seen you like this . . . so upset." My reply was simple, "You've never seen me immediately after a parent-teacher conference." My thoughts, however, went something like this: "My poor baby, how are you ever going to feel good about yourself when you've got a lousy mother and you've got a teacher who not only thinks you're a real dud, but humiliates *you* to prove a point." Oh, my . . . we lousy moms can just hurt all over for our hurt children, but we're so inept we can't do what we should to keep them from hurting. And this, the school, is Mom's conscience, but it doesn't do wonders for her self-esteem, without which it gets pretty difficult to improve as a mother.

I've long tried to follow my pediatrician's advice about Lisa's thumb-sucking, a not-unheard-of habit in a seven-year-old. He says to ignore it. But after that dreadful meeting with the teacher, I conjured up a picture of my poor little girl sitting up in front of the class feeling grossly self-conscious, vigorously sucking her thumb, kids giggling at her, viewing her as some sort of freak. And I felt guilty and sad. I felt guilty that Lisa sucks her thumb, not because it offends me, but because she must feel insecure; I felt guilty about dragging my feet over her glasses, and had really planned on getting them that day while my friend was so generously carting me about, and oh, I just plain felt guilty, inadequate, and sad.

The detail, trivia, and tedium that attend child-rearing build up to the point where the total task of adequate mothering seems most formidable—because of minutiae. We—myself and the many mothers who shared their views with me—become overwhelmed by an accumulation of small obligations and enormous responsibilities, and we very often retreat from the whole of the combination. Now, of course, after the meeting, I was feeling that all the tiny transgressions were symptoms of overall benign neglect.

Before I had children I smugly thought that mothers overreacted to parent-teacher conferences. My sister, for instance, seemed to spend half her life at the school and the rest of it brooding about her children's problems. After meetings with her kids' teachers she always seemed depressed or agitated. *I*, on the other hand, would take matters more in stride once *I* was a mother. Now I know what it's like to be called over to the school because "Lisa doesn't jump rope as well as Sally and Karen," because she

116

sucks her thumb, chews her hair, talks too loud, laughs too much, doesn't talk, doesn't laugh. And Adam. "He's too intelligent, Mrs. Radl; he said 'shit' seven times in four days, talked back three days ago, hit Bobby with his lunch box, and doesn't trike at trike time."

I know how it feels to be told by a teacher how my children are or aren't doing—it gets you in the gut. And I'm just starting out, and understand that so far I've had it really easy.

Many middle-class mothers I talked to had real horror stories that made my experiences as the mother of school-children seem trivial by comparison. It is bad enough that we must insecurely ask teachers' advice; that frequently the advice we are given proves so far off the mark is terrifying.

One mother told this story:

> My daughter, who is now a straight-A student in college, was judged by her second-grade teacher to be extremely slow. I was frantic, thinking of course that the girl was retarded, but after I calmed down I realized that I knew my daughter pretty well, and she could, after all, read quite well—not exactly a symptom that supported the notion that she was either slow or retarded. I just let matters slide, and she did quite well in school, much to the surprise and, I suspect somehow, the dismay of her teacher. But then, a couple of years later, the school nurse and one of her teachers got me in a corner and talked to me about Sarah's speech impediment—she lisped. They recommended that she have surgery. I agonized over that, but decided to wait. After I had her teeth straightened, the lisp disappeared without surgery, and I realized that I had been right in thinking that it's pretty difficult to articulate when one's teeth are parallel to the floor. She's fine now—very fine—but these are only two incidents where the school could have guided me into erroneous decisions that might have marked my daughter for life.

The mother of a little boy, eight years old, told me

that she was already regretting her decision to go along with her son's teacher when it was suggested that the boy be held back in the first grade. The child was not a slow learner, but the teacher gave his immaturity as the basis for her recommendation. Where once the child was simply immature, he is now failing miserably in all of his subjects, and in view of his past performance, this is indeed a surprise. As a pre-schooler and first-grader, he was a fast learner, seeming to grasp skills more quickly than most children his age. He has a marked talent for drawing and painting, a fine sense of humor, and more recently has shown apparent ability at the piano. These are not exactly the qualities possessed by a dumb kid, but he is simply not learning anything at school. He has no self-confidence, and he had recently started to feign illness to get his mother to keep him home from school. His present teacher and his mother are at wit's end. The teacher has recommended that the mother get in touch with the school psychologist. She has tried to do so for months, and has been unable to reach him. The last time we spoke, she indicated that she would take the boy to a private counselor. She expressed doubt that they'd find an answer, but she could not just stand by and do nothing.

Another mother I know has harbored a deep guilt for years because she did not follow the advice of her son's fifth-grade teacher and seek professional help. The boy is now in his twenties and married. He is having marital difficulties, and his mother wonders if that might have been prevented if she had heeded the advice of the all-knowing teacher. Think for a minute how crowded the offices of psychiatrists and therapists would be if everyone who has marital difficulties, or might have in the future, were in treatment.

"The school experts told me that my son was hopelessly mentally retarded and recommended that we put him in a special school," said the mother of four children. The experts advised this boy's hand-wringing parents that he would never progress beyond the first-grade level, or that of a six-year-old. The child's first-grade teacher gave the mother the name and address of a "place for this kind

118

of child"; the mother visited it, she became physically ill, and then she just sobbed. She took him to doctors, psychiatrists, and counselors, and finally learned from the boy himself that whenever the class was to have a spelling or math test, the teacher didn't give him and two other children the material to study because she only gave out the study tools to those she had determined could actually do the work. After two years of utter misery and many bizarre experiences this poor woman put her son in a private school. He's no Albert Einstein, but he *did* graduate from high school and go on to vocational school.

The most extreme case I have heard was that of a boy in his first year of junior college. The dean looked him right in the eye and said, "Your I.Q. is under 80; obviously you cannot continue attending classes here." If it were not wild enough that the dean felt the boy could comprehend that statement, add to it this: The young man in question was graduated with honors and then picked up a master's degree in education at Stanford University. Stanford is hardly regarded as a school for mental defectives.

Educator John Holt cites an example, one that is only the tip of the iceberg, of extremes in parent-teacher interaction. He tells the story of an acquaintance of his who, in a state of agitation, came to him for advice. The man had a friend who was having a terrible problem with her child at school. The child was getting good enough marks, but he was behaving so badly that he disrupted the entire class. The teacher had already called the mother several times, and it had been suggested that the child be taken to a psychologist and perhaps be given drugs. Holt describes the man as emphasizing that the mother was growing frantic, and the school was demanding that something be done:

> . . . with visions of a thirteen- or fourteen-year-old boy on the rampage, hitting out in all directions, I said, "How old is the child?" His wife said, "He is six."
> "Six!" I thought to myself, what in the world can a six-year-old do in the classroom that can throw all

119

these adults into such a panic. . . . What this six-year-old was doing to cause such an uproar was only this —he likes to get up out of his seat from time to time and go talk to his friends. He refuses to stay seated. At first, I could hardly believe my ears. Was it really no more than that? Apparently, that was all. Otherwise, as my friend described him, the child was lively, sociable, attractive, and had many friends.

My friend said to me, "We think the child may be hyperactive." I assured him, on the basis of what he had told me, that he was almost certainly not "hyperactive," and that in any case, such a diagnosis could only be made by a very few highly specialized people on the basis of elaborate tests which the child had not been given. There was no question at all of the child hitting other children . . . throwing tantrums. He just likes to talk to people: I tried to convince my friend that the only problem was that this lively, energetic, and personable kid had had the bad luck, like many other kids, to get a first-grade teacher who like many other teachers believed that six-year-olds ought to spend a very large part of their waking hours sitting down, motionless, and quiet. . . . This child may all too soon find his way into the hands of experts who will find something they can say is wrong with him. . . . (A month later, I learned that he was being given drugs, which have "solved the problem.")[2]

John Holt and the Birds did not relieve my paranoia about elementary school teachers as much as talking to a young married couple—teachers and parents themselves. The young woman summed up the advice she constantly gives to parents: "Just tell the teacher you agree completely, admire him/her greatly, and will leave no stone unturned to comply with his/her recommendations. Volunteer for everything, and then beg off with a sick headache—in fact, sometimes when you volunteer to do something, you will find no one will ever follow up, and you're off the hook."

Her husband had this to say: "I watch my co-workers get a charge out of making parents feel rotten about both themselves and their kids—they really do enjoy it, you know. Where else can they wield such power?"

"Just wait till the kids are in school—things will be easier," we're told when we're wrestling with infants, diaper pails, and the bother of pre-schoolers. Many women would gladly take back the diapers, the formula, and the innocent mischief of toddlers—because once they're old enough to go to school, there's a whole new dimension of responsibility, more than teacher conferences, the PTA, homework, or scouts. That new weight of responsibility involves the molding of minds and morals, and it is open-ended.

School with all of its activities is less telling than the fact that babies and little children grow up—that growing process is the real work of parents, with no end in sight until we finally see our children safely to adulthood.

I could indict the school, and suggest that they dispense with all extra-curricular activities—if not for me, then for mothers like Mrs. L. But that is not really the problem. It is not the school's fault our kids start growing up—that is what life is all about.

It is about, for mothers anyway, guiding your children —from toilet-training right up through making sure you've instilled in them enough proper values to keep them from stealing cars or destroying their minds with drugs, through seeing them grown steady and healthy enough to make the right choices on their own for the rest of their lives.

7

Molding young 🌺 minds and morals

In one widely read book on child behavior, the authors tell us that some three-year-olds enjoy wandering about the house late at night while the family sleeps, exploring places and things, perhaps getting something to eat from the refrigerator, and maybe sleeping the rest of the night on the living room sofa. . . . We agree there are some three-year-olds who might enjoy such nocturnal adventures, but the authors then go on to tell the concerned parents that this is really nothing to be concerned about. All the parents need do is to make sure the front door and back door are locked so the child can't wander out into the street. And put the knives and poisons out of reach. This may be normal expected behavior of the three-year-old, but what the experts don't tell you is the normal expected behavior of the three-year-old's mother as she cleans up the mess of spilled milk, sugar, breakfast cereal, and tries to remove the lipstick he has used to decorate the living room wall.

—Power to the Parents
JOSEPH AND LOIS BIRD
(DOUBLEDAY, 1972)

WHEN MY CHILDREN were babies, I saw Dr. Lendon Smith, "The Children's Doctor," on a television talk show. He said that toilet-training was unnecessary, that if the parents used the bathroom, the children would follow their example and use it, too. I took his advice and it worked for us. I didn't have to spend hours in the bathroom and in discussions of the subject with my little kids, there were very few accidents to take care of in training pants, and a lot of wear and tear was saved on my nerves and perhaps on the psyches of my children. But sticking to my plan was difficult.

For one thing, it was so easy I felt that I was copping out. For another, I had lots of advice. To accomplish this "non-training," a mother is told to keep her child in diapers until he lets her know that he no longer needs to wear them. So here I had a two-year-old still in her diapers. I could put my kids through college if I had a dollar for every time I head the questions, "Is that child *still* in diapers? When *are* you going to train her? Have you read Spock?"

A friend of mine followed Spock—or rather she tried to. Spock, like other experts, states that children will be trained first to have bowel movements, and afterward learn to urinate in the toilet. My friend's child did just the reverse, and it dove her nearly mad. Since the child had skipped phase one and moved right into phase two, she was confused about how to proceed and she feared that her son might just never return to phase one.

To the inexperienced mother, striving to do well and to do the best for her child, the conflicting views of the child-guidance experts and the well-meaning advice of friends ("My Stevie was trained at a year") and grandparents ("Your sister was trained at four months") on everything from toilet-training to the best brand of baby food serves only to confuse. Raising a child is an extraordinarily complex and challenging job and, not only are most new mothers completely uneducated for it, their on-the-job training is almost always conducted with advice that is neither useful nor helpful.

It is hard enough to make your way through raising babies; it is even worse when the children's problems go beyond what come to be remembered as simple little matters.

A friend of mine, the mother of four girls, once remarked. "When things get bad, and I don't know how to handle a particular situation with one of the children, I often sit down and read Spock, Ginott, or Salk. After a half hour's reading, I feel better. I still don't have an answer, but the momentary escape of reading distracts me enough to carry me over the frustration and rage I feel on such occasions."

One child-guidance specialist has yet to provide me with the answers to my questions on discipline, but he never fails to entertain and amuse me. He tells us that when a child throws a cherished object across the room and smashes it to smithereens, a mother should say calmly, "Things are not for throwing. Balls are for throwing," and then calmly hand the child a ball.

Our delightful specialist also advises that when a child mischievously breaks a window, a mother should say calmly, "Windows are not for breaking." When I look at the jagged shards of a plate glass window, I must admit that my sense of humor and good will fail me.

One widely read manual tells us that the best way to make sure our children understand what is expected of them is to talk it over with them at length.

Another well-known manual advises that parents mustn't become argumentative and verbose, nor should they give long explanations. The author winds it up by saying, "If the parent talks too much, he conveys weakness—at a time when he must convey strength."

Not only do the experts disagree among themselves tending to confuse and bewilder parents, but it is not unusual for an expert to contradict himself.

A very famous pediatrician tells us that threats tend to weaken discipline, and suggests for example that we avoid threatening to take away a child's bike to keep him from riding it in the street. Then goes on to say that if such drastic action must be taken, a parent should give a child fair warning. How is one to differentiate between a "threat" and a "warning"?

Since the children have left the what-do-you-do-for-teething-pain stage, every time I have looked for an answer to a particular problem in my eleven different child-rearing manuals, I have been left with the feeling that our children's problems must fall outside the normal range and that, with its varying moods and emotions, our household is totally abnormal. Four people and one dog live here; playmates drift in and out; salesmen and friends call up and come by, some people are shaving while other people are dressing, some people are cleaning up breakfast dishes or emptying the garbage, while others are getting ready to go to the office or to school. Some days it rains, some days the TV goes out, some days someone is sick, some days dinner is late. I have come away from these manuals with the feeling that the people who read them must be mothers of one child (or mothers who never find themselves with more than one child at a time needing attention). That mother's sole function is to serve and guide, that she is devoid of any emotion save overwhelming love for that one child who has just committed that one act on that one page of that one manual. (That father lurks in the background where he provides vague support and encouragement for the mother, and brings home money.) The family lives in a world where events never converge, no variables are involved in the care of the children, life

127

remains stable, and the perpetual backdrop is an enormous white room in which mother and child do nothing but interact.

If the experts agree on one thing, it is that parents should be "consistent" in their discipline and guidance. "Consistency," however, is a state of perfection, and perfection is not a human condition. Perhaps it can exist in the sterile world of the child-rearing manuals, but it doesn't work in real life.

One day a child can break a glass, and his mother will say, "That's okay, accidents happen." On another day, when the washing machine has gone out, the children have been misbehaving, the phone has been ringing, she's had a bad session with her son's teacher, and one of the kids has broken her glasses when he should not have had his hands on them, she will fly into a rage at the final assault on both her senses and her possessions. A mother, not being a robot, is incapable of consistency.

The range of problems a mother must deal with in guiding children goes from the absurd and trivial to the very serious. How she handles a given situation depends not only on the gravity of the problem but on a great many variables.

Every year, for instance, we send out pictures of the kids with our Christmas cards. And every year I find myself idiotically telling the kids, "Smile or I'll tan your hides." Yet, when one of them has done something *far* more serious than not smiling for a photograph, my attitude can, depending on the circumstances, be considerably more tolerant.

We have a steadfast rule that children *must* come directly home from the bus stop to check in and change their clothes. This rule is for their safety and my peace of mind. Lisa broke the rule for the first time recently, and was lost for three hours. I called the school and all of her playmates' homes. Then I combed the neighborhood. With growing panic, I called the police. Before the squad car arrived, I saw her. Tears were streaming down her face. I could see that whatever was troubling her was deeper than the prospect of a confrontation with an angry

128

and scared mother. What should I do? Admonish her for being late when she was already obviously miserable? If I did, would I ever find out what was troubling her so I could help?

By asking her what was wrong, I found out where she had been, but she was still so hurt I didn't have the heart to discipline her for not coming straight home. She had gone to play with a girl who had just moved into the neighborhood and some older kids had started calling her "four eyes," teasing her about her glasses.

I was distressed that she had disobeyed an important rule and caused me to worry horribly, but I could still feel her hurt. And I was disturbed that the teasing would counteract all I had done to ensure that she regularly wear her glasses. I'm confident that I handled things properly, but every time I let an infraction of important rules slip by, I feel uneasy because I have been inconsistent.

No child-rearing manual tells you how to deal with everyday problems like the one that came up the other day.

Adam and Lisa and two friends were planning a carnival in our back yard to raise funds for muscular dystrophy. Realizing how important it was to them that it be their very own project, I resolved not to interfere. The four children set about cleaning the patio area and putting everything in shape, and in their excitement "forgot" my warning not to move the marble table (partly because it is too heavy, and partly because they might drop and break it). After they had been working for about an hour, the four little kids appeared in the doorway, eyes cast downward.

"We're sorry. We forgot. We dropped the table." They disobeyed me, and it's hard to believe that all four didn't remember the warning. But what do you say to kids who are trying to raise money to help kids less fortunate than themselves? Feeling sad at the loss of the first piece of furniture my husband and I bought when we were newlyweds, I said, "It's okay, kids, don't worry about it."

Again I feel that I handled the situation properly and

that most mothers would do the same. But I was certainly inconsistent.

Whether it's determining what sort of toilet-training methods to use or deciding what to do about a teenage daughter's contraception, in the end we are alone. The experts do not help us, and the responsibilities are harrowing. How do you instill values? How do you answer youngsters' millions of questions intelligently? How do you, in short, make yourself a good mother? What counts, what doesn't count, what is your job, what is the school's job, and what is best left to chance? How do you ensure that they will grow up to be decent and content human beings? In our society the care and training of children is the mother's responsibility. And mothers find it an onerous one.

It is the nature of our society to blame the parents for the behavior of the child. Teenagers who misbehave are assumed to have been badly raised. And it is in the nature of mothers to blame themselves when they see their teenagers presenting staggering problems.

Four years ago, Bea became overwrought about the long hair on her two teenage sons. She didn't know what to do. She didn't really understand why she felt so upset, because it didn't bother her when other boys let their hair grow down to their shoulders. She sought refuge by pointing to them, rolling her eyes and hastily saying, "I can't talk about it." When her older son dropped out of college, she became depressed and again didn't know what to do. She feared that if she urged him to return, he would become more determined to stay out; but then she feared that if she didn't encourage him, she'd miss an opportunity to reason with him, to show him why this was a mistake. But this time, he was twenty-one years old, and legally an adult. Should she throw him out of the house? He was, after all, an adult. But then he was her son. The question remained unresolved for her, and another cropped up. Would her sixteen-year-old follow in the same path? She had failed one of her children; would she fail the other? Would she fail completely in the one thing that had been her life's work—motherhood?

Theresa seemed terribly distraught that her nineteen-year-old son had dropped out of college. Finally she said, "If that were all there was to it, I'd be grateful. He didn't really drop out voluntarily. We brought him home. He's sick. He started smoking a little grass a few months ago and then became interested in hallucinogens. Apparently, he and several of his friends started experimenting with mescaline. We had no idea until we received a call from one of his roommates telling us he'd been hospitalized. From what we're told by both our son and the hospital officials, he took an LSD trip, and it was a bad one—or, as the kids say, a bummer. He seems so strange now. I fear he is damaged for life. And I keep wondering where I went wrong."

The mother of an eighteen-year-old boy, a boy she had ambitious plans for—Stanford University, a law career, a credit to the family, himself, and her as a mother: "He's running wild, and there is nothing we can do. He dropped out of high school, and legally that's his right. He goes off with his friends and doesn't come back for days at a time. Sometimes he seems normal, other times I can tell that he's 'on' something. All our plans—down the drain. His father has washed his hands of him completely."

"Nowadays," said the mother of two teenage girls, "it's harder to deal with teenagers. Sometimes I think I'm too strict, and I know that I'm not 'with it' about sex and drugs, but honestly I don't want my daughters to wind up dope fiends or pregnant. Right now, one of the girls is 'in love' with a bum. I don't let her go out with him, but how do I know she won't sneak around to see him because she has such a crush on him? How do I know that he won't talk her into something? Sure she has values, but I remember what 'first love' was like, and it can be a pretty strong influence on a young girl. Sometimes I panic. The same things that work with one of my daughters don't work with the other. And you can only hope that the years of trying to mold their values has some effect. But if they fall in with the wrong kids, it doesn't seem to matter whether you've done a good job. Sometimes I fear that my strictness will cause a reaction, and yet I fear that if I'm permissive, it will be less than nothing. It's damned if you do, and damned if you don't."

A father laments, "You get them through it. You finally get them through the mumps, measles, elementary school, homework, scouts, high school, the fights over staying out late, using the car, drinking beer, experimenting with pot. He's a good clean kid, after all, thank God. And then he goes out and smashes himself up on a motorcycle. He'll live, but you should see what he did to what was once his face."

Answering the myriad questions that little children ask can be exhilarating sometimes. At times it can be infuriating. When you're trying to add up a bank statement and your child asks you why the grass is green, it's hard not to succumb to a feeling of annoyance. How much must I do to keep me from feeling that I'm failing my children in some way? How much time can I take for myself without feeling selfish, without feeling that I'm neglecting them, without feeling that they may sense a rejection of them on my part? How much "enrichment" is enough? If I don't particularly want to go to the zoo or to the museum, am I causing them to suffer in some way? The children themselves offer little feedback. Mothers are frequently distressed when children fail to appreciate utterly the nice things that are done for them. It simply isn't human to be totally selfless. And because there's no way to look into the future and behold your child at twenty-five and feel assured that you've done a good job of raising him, the doubts and fears abound.

As they grow, there are teeth to be brushed, toys to be picked up, social amenities to be observed, and millions of things to learn. While all of this is going on, children, being the wonderfully curious creatures they are, get up on roofs, climb trees, take things apart, and generally get into one hell of a lot of mischief in the process of learning about their world.

And as they grow and learn, so must we. Each day brings surprises—instant tests for us to pass or fail. And each child is a brand-new experience with foibles all his own.

One mother, whose four children range from seven to eighteen years, finds herself dismayed at both the experts and herself. "You'd think I'd know pretty well how to handle most situations by now, but I don't. Each child is entirely different in temperament, intelligence, and interests. If my oldest daughter, for example, asks permission to do something, and I want to give it some thought before I answer, she accepts my decision. But the next child in line not only continues to argue her case, but a final 'no' answer is construed by her as a 'maybe,' and a 'maybe' as a 'yes.' I had always assumed that my first child would be my most difficult because essentially I'd practice there and bring vast experience to my caring for and guiding subsequent children. That just hasn't happened. Whatever I learn with each of them, other than the basics, applies only to each on an individual basis. I'm sure if I had another child, guidance would be just as much of a mystery to me as it always has been."

The father of six children says this: "Try hopping back and forth between the problems of a college freshman and a four-year-old. It's schizophrenic."

"My husband," said Eleanor, the mother of two boys, nine and five, "drives me up the wall with his running commentary on how I raise the kids."

He comes home quite late, sees the children only on weekends, really. They are, in the curious way of children, quite good when he's around. It's funny, isn't it, how they're so good and well behaved with baby-sitters and relatives and Daddy. Every woman I know has commented on the way you'll walk in the door, be congratulated by the sitter on how adorable and easy-to-get-along-with your children are, and then, five minutes after the door is shut behind her, be in the middle of deciding which one to hit over the head first. On the occasions the children are difficult and

133

balky and I feel called upon to discipline them, my husband will tell me that I'm really not doing it at all well. If I yell at them, he'll suggest that it would work far better to reason with them. If I reason with them, he'll pitch in with his opinion that I'm not being strict enough with them, and that what they really need is a spanking. Of course, the insidious thing is that I always feel that he may be right. If my childless great-aunt whom I haven't seen in twenty years butts in with her ideas on child-rearing I think she may be right. Spock may be right, and all the other experts may be right. Anyone, in fact, can be right, because I certainly can't say that I am. Sometimes one thing works and sometimes another thing works. Sometimes I think I'm doing the right thing, and sometimes I know perfectly well I'm doing the wrong thing. And the whole time I'm dealing with them, I feel totally inadequate to the task—totally unhelped by any of the experts. When I consider myself to have punished them rather too severely, I feel guilty as hell. What am I doing to their little psyches if, on Monday, Tuesday, and Wednesday I say nothing about their smearing paint on the play-room floor, but on Thursday I come in and give them a thorough dressing down because Thursday has been a dreadful day and I've just come home from the dentist? Most disciplinary situations are not covered in Spock. It's quite easy to decide that you'll punish your child if he takes something from a store, or deliberately breaks something. But what do you do when he's fighting with his brother and you think, but you're not entirely sure, that he's at fault. Punish one? Punish both? Leave them alone? And what about those times when something gets broken purely by accident? And that thing happens to be something that you valued quite highly? Sometimes you can be quite rational and shrug it off and say something along the lines of "Please be more careful." Other times your impulse is considerably less reasoned. And you scream or you spank or you take away television privileges for three days because you're only human and you're angry and you're lashing out in anger.

Ann, who has three daughters, ages eleven, eight, and four, puts it this way:

I think I'd been a mother for about two weeks when I realized why parents spoil children. It's so much easier that way. Just give them what they want and they'll stop bothering you. I remember when my first child was a baby. If she cried it seemed much easier to give her another bottle. But that led to the problem of whether that was good or bad for her. Would she expect it all the time? Was she getting spoiled? What was better—to feed her or to let her cry? I remember vowing before I had kids that I'd never bribe them and I'd never threaten them. And after being a mother for eleven years I've discovered that the only things that seem to work are bribes and threats—and every mother I've ever spoken to has admitted that the only things that work are bribes and threats. But every time I say, "If you clean up your rooms I'll let you have lollipops," I have the guilty feeling that I'm doing the wrong thing—that I'm not giving them the proper outlook on life.

Kathryn, the mother of a son age nine and a daughter age seven, is concerned with spoiling her children:

The very word "spoiled" says an awful lot. It implies that you'll do something to make them not good. Of course my children are spoiled—for one thing, because I work I'm less likely to be hard on them. I'm with them such a relatively small amount of time that I want that time to be pleasant for them. I don't want it to be full of "nos" and "you can'ts." Also, because I work, I think they're rather spoiled in terms of material possessions. I buy them things and take them places out of a sense of guilt to make up to them for my working. I suppose in the end my problem, and that of a lot of mothers I know, is that I want my children to like me. And how can they like me if I keep doing things to them that they don't like? On the other hand, I'm constantly concerned that they are being spoiled, that they're growing up with the wrong set of values. But, when I stop to think of how one goes about instilling values, I'm totally at sea. We live in an age where some of the experts speak out for permissiveness and other experts call for strictness. We've all heard enough for and against both sides to make us confused. To say that I should just do what comes naturally is absurd. What seems natural one day seems totally unnatural the next. I laugh when I hear about consistency. And yet, my concern is with the responsibility I hold for molding them. If anyone had asked me before I had children to write a five-hundred-word essay on how precisely to mold children, I'd have been at a complete loss. It simply didn't occur to me that the responsibility would be as great as it is. And I'm still at a loss. I do what most other mothers do—I do what I can and I pray for the best. But I'm never quite free of the nagging worry that my best is far from good enough.

One woman zeroed in on the unpleasantness of actually carrying out discipline: "One of the nicest things about going away alone with my husband is that I spend the entire time saying, 'Yes, let's do that,' or 'Yes, why don't you,' or 'Yes, I'd love to,' in rather sharp contrast to the constant 'nos' I deal out at home. I suppose there are a hundred reasons why I like to go away alone with my husband, but one of them is certainly that I feel a hell of a lot less rigid as a person. I'm not a person who likes to discipline and deny. My husband has pointed out quite accurately that when we're away from the kids even my voice sounds different—it's younger and warmer and considerably more pleasant."

Ellen, the mother of two girls, now grown, reminisced about raising them:

The thing I remember the best is how terrible I felt when I'd do things I'd sworn not to do. I suppose I was particularly sensitive to that because I'd hated the way my mother had raised me—I remember how unfair I thought it was when she punished me totally out of proportion. Once she practically beat me up because I'd pulled down some curtains, completely by accident. And yet, I'd find myself behaving in an equally irra-ational way with my children. I'd vowed to be rational, reasonable, sensible, and fair with them in a way my mother had never been with me. I found myself being totally unreasonable and unfair more times than I care to recall. I remember thinking how stupid it was of her to buy me off—how demeaning, almost. And then I'd find myself buying my children off. I remember how, before I had kids, I'd see mothers in super-markets shame their kids into tears, scream at them, behave in an absolutely vulgar, disgusting, and alto-gether unreasonable way. I remember thinking how I'd absolutely never, ever, ever do anything like that. But I did. And I had young women look at me in the same way I'd looked at mothers before I'd had kids. But the thing that galls me the most is how I assumed I'd be so much better a mother than my mother was to me—and how I wasn't. Now my older daughter is pregnant and I wonder what promises she's making to herself that she's going to find herself breaking in a couple of years.

The frustration, pain, guilt, and fear accompanying what we not-so-rational mothers inflict on our children in the name of training and discipline is well illustrated in the following letter included in *Between Parent and Child* by Dr. Haim Ginott:

If I leave anything unsaid I know that you will be able to read between the lines. You were very kind to come to our church to conduct a discussion group for parents. While it was not completely satisfactory to me because I never learn enough on the subject of raising children, one thing that appealed to me was the statement that you knew that no parents deliberately did things to injure their children emotionally. Rather, they did so unwittingly. Not one of us willingly would do anything to cripple our children spiritually, morally, or emotionally, and yet we do just that. I cry often inside for things I have done and said thoughtlessly

137

and I pray not to repeat these transgressions. Maybe they aren't repeated but something else just as bad is substituted, until I am frantic for fear that I have injured my child for life.

This letter struck a familiar chord. How many times I've felt that I've really hurt the children, how many times I actually have hurt them, I do not know. I only know that I've done nearly everything on my mental I-will-never list. I'm bitterly amused when I reflect on my attitude before I had the kids. I was very quick to say and think, "But it will be different with me."

8

Spare the rod

IN RECOGNIZING that parents are capable occasionally of anger, Dr. Spock says:

> Sometimes it takes a long time to realize that you are losing your temper. The child may have been putting on a series of irritating acts from the time he appeared at breakfast—making disagreeable remarks about the food, half deliberately knocking over a glass of milk, playing with something forbidden and breaking it, picking on a younger child—all of which you have tried to ignore in a supreme effort to be patient. Then at the final act, which perhaps isn't so bad, your resentment suddenly boils over, and it shocks you a little with its vehemence. Often when you look back over such a series of exasperating actions, you can see that the child has been asking for firmness or punishment all morning and that it was your well-intentioned efforts at overpatience that made him go from one provocation to another, looking for a check.[1]

But he doesn't tell us what to *do* about it. Nobody does. And nobody explains that sometimes it isn't that a parent is intentionally ignoring a child, but instead has temporarily tuned the child out, and is suddenly brought back to attention while everything has been working on her at a subconscious level.

"I watch with horror as I behave in a manner diametrically opposed to my most profound beliefs. One day after I had just had it up to here with everything, I sprawled out on the sofa to relax with the newspaper. As I sat there, wearing my peace medallion and lamenting all of the violence in the world, the kids started scuffling while watching TV. After the boy hit the girl, I jumped up and belted him, yelling, *'Stop hitting, I can't stand violence.'* " This confession came from a sweet, easy-going father of two young children—a Methodist minister who counsels those with family problems.

One friend, the mother of three boys, got so angry when her oldest son broke a new toy, she threw all of his little cars and trucks on the patio and jumped up and down on them until they were in pieces. The boy just looked on aghast while she told him, "If you can't respect your toys then you can't have them."

The mother of a teenage girl admits that she broke a bed while chasing her daughter around the room in an effort to mete out disciplinary action because the girl had just hurled insults at her. The broken bed only inflamed her more. What had pushed her beyond the limit was that she had tried to teach her daughter respect, and felt, at least momentarily, that it had all been in vain.

Psychologist Haim Ginott also recognizes that parents get angry—

> When we lose our temper, we act as though we had lost our sanity. We say and do things to our children that we would hesitate to inflict on an enemy. We yell, insult, and hit below the belt. When the fanfare is over, we feel guilty and we solemnly resolve never to render a repeat performance. But anger soon strikes again, undoing our good intentions. Once more we lash out at those to whose welfare we have dedicated our life and fortune.[2]

Fine. But how do we handle it? How do we keep from behaving like lunatics when our kids are just begging for discipline? Why do they beg? Is it for attention? What, if not the spanking they are asking for, do we give them? Will just ordinary attention do the trick? If we don't really let them have it, will we be too permissive, and therefore damage them emotionally? When we are enraged, how do we call upon remembered advice?

I once saw one of the best mothers I know slap her child across the face while hovering over him in rage, totally shaken at what she considered absolutely intolerable behavior. It was a painful sight. What made it even more painful was that although the child looked healthy and normal, he was terminally ill. The agony in this mother's face will always be etched in my memory.

I am no match for this brave and magnificent mother, but we have in common that we detest this form of discipline. We are both nonviolent and share the view that face-slapping robs people of their dignity. It would seem to be impossible that anything could happen that would make us subject our children—of all people—to such humiliation.

A few weeks ago I slapped my young daughter across the face for balking at taking a bath. Moments later, the remorse, love, and empathy for her hurt and humiliation welled up in me painfully. My guilt was completely deserved because she had merely triggered an explosion that had been building for hours. Ironically, Adam had been particularly obnoxious a few moments before and was dealt with appropriately. But Lisa took the brunt because her act was the final trivial incident of that particulalr day. I was pushed beyond my tolerance level.

I know very well how important it is to gently, but firmly, push a child in the right direction and that very often counting to ten, making him stand in the corner, or sending him to his room can get the desired results. And yet all too often, this reasonable method of dealing with misbehaving children is completely forgotten when Mom's simply had enough of their arguing, nagging, shouting, or back talk. And the fuse gets shorter as the physical and emotional fatigue gets longer. My own behavior in these instances doesn't do much for my self-respect, but at the moment of rage, Benjamin Spock is a complete stranger and my self-respect is not even under consideration.

Where were my reason and self-respect on that lovely Sunday afternoon last December when I told them I was leaving them for good—that they'd just have to find another mommy—and put on my coat and walked out the door? Did I do that? Unbelievable.

After I had done the dishes, made the beds, and stuffed a load of clothes in the washer, Daddy tripped off to run some errands, the children went out to play, and I sat down to work on a project that was hanging fire. Minutes later the kids were back in the house, asking for potato chips and chocolate milk while pulling on the Christmas tree and mutilating several packages. Correcting the situation, I returned to my project, but before I got settled down, they started wrestling on the living room floor, knocked over an ashtray, and kicked the antique carved chest. After I meted out the appropriate punishment, they became very quiet.

While I was congratulating myself on my disciplinary expertise, the silence was broken by the sound of a quart of milk hitting the newly waxed kitchen floor. And from that point on things continued to deteriorate until I finally exploded. I spanked them, put them to bed, and announced I was leaving. I stalked out of the house amid mournful sobbing and pleading and frightened questions about who would take care of them.

Oh, I came back. In five minutes I was back in the house muttering something about having forgotten money for bus fare. They begged me to stay. The rest of the day and evening they were little angels.

That I could be driven to demonstrate such utter hostility and hatred, making those two little beloved children insecure in the process, is despicable.

A letter from a suffering mother, appearing in a "Dear Abby" column also hit home. The woman wrote that she had hollered like a fishwife at her ten-year-old daughter as she was leaving for school. She went on to say that it was over a trivial matter, that she was so ashamed of herself, and that her daughter's feelings were obviously hurt.

143

The woman was sick at heart at her action and felt pain for her hurt child.

I've been there, too. I have sent off not one but two children to face the day feeling bad about themselves. One morning when I was trying to get Adam and Lisa ready for school, they kept dawdling, and the clock kept ticking away. I was tired, I prodded them to eat their breakfast, get their clothes on, and get moving so they could get to the bus stop on time. Finally, I blew my top.

After things cooled off, and I had bid them good-bye, I watched them walk off, hand-in-hand, heads lowered, knowing that their day had started with them holding back tears—not exactly a good way to start the day.

My God, what a terrible mother. And although I re- call how bad I felt that day, I have repeated the same thing. It happens despite my feelings that the morning sets the tone for the entire day and, just as bedtime is a time for kissing and making up, the beginning of the day should be happy.

When my children become targets for my wrath, I try to find comfort in the words of Dr. Ginott:

> There is a place for parental anger in child education. In fact, failure to get angry at certain moments would only convey to the child indifference, not goodness. Those who care cannot altogether shun anger . . .[3]

But I can't relieve my guilty fears.

The irrational behavior of parents, particularly moth- ers, is sometimes humorous, often sad, and—many of us fear—emotionally damaging to small children. But what is even more disturbing is a parental reaction that none of us is prepared for, and when that happens, it strikes terror in our hearts.

A good friend and former co-worker, Bill, the father of three boys, startled me with his honesty. Bill is an un- usual father—it's not just Little League, PTA, or scouts— he really helps. When they were babies, he would get up for middle-of-the-night feedings, change their diapers, bathe them, and put them to bed. As they grew, this kind

144

of participation continued—an unusual, sensitive, and loving father.

One day we were chatting, and naturally the conversation got around to his boys. Quite suddenly Bill said, "There's a fine line between honest discipline and child abuse, and it's frightening how often I find myself at the threshold of crossing over." This came from a man who is gentle and kind and who loves his children deeply.

My own way of handling things has been to walk away when I felt my head filling dangerously with rage— rage I never expected to experience; before I had children I had been virtually devoid of a temper. In fact, I cannot remember ever hitting another person in anger—even when I was a child. Perhaps "walk away" is not honest. I have *run* from the house more than once because I was genuinely afraid that if I laid a hand on one of the kids, it wouldn't stop there. I have reached the threshold of violence only a few times, and the sheer terror of my own rage has kept things in check.

Years ago I watched my gentle mother kick a box around the kitchen for several minutes—she was so enraged at my younger brother that, as she kicked the box, she called to my father to "get him out of my sight—if I touch him I'll kill him." She meant it. Yet she adored my brother, and she was never one to spank any of us very much.

Another woman, a seemingly sane one, broke several yardsticks over her son in fits of rage. After a time her fury and guilt showed up as muscle spasms so severe she would occasionally pass out. Fortunately, she has never really harmed her child—physically.

A friend of mine regularly hurls her cat across the back yard. She confesses that at times, she, peace-loving, gentle, and nonviolent, has such feelings of hostility toward her children that she dares not discipline them for fear of where it might lead. She has reasoned that it is better to throw a cat across the yard than to throw a child out the window.

Scores of mothers, and a few fathers, have confessed to coming very close to battering a child, to momentarily feeling such anger, hating a child so much, that maiming or killing him would be almost a pleasure. These parents have held their emotions in check and while they have not hurt their children physically they have built up a never-ending storehouse of guilt, shame, self-hatred, and fear—fear that just once they won't stop at the threshold, but will slip slightly over.

Janet has slipped over, and it's not clear whether or not she knows it. She is the upper-middle-class mother of two children, and she openly confessed that she had solved what she considered a rather sticky problem.

When her children were pre-schoolers she liked to sleep late in the morning, but the kids had other ideas. The two little demons would scramble out of bed at about 7 o'clock each morning, climb into bed with Mama, cry, make noise, and get into mischief. The innovative young mother got around this by tying her youngsters spread-eagled to their beds, shutting off the sounds of their crying with a series of closed doors. She would release them (several hours later) when she had gotten enough sleep. She proudly stated that after they'd gotten the idea, the *fear* that she would do just that was enough to keep them in line.

Janet is a nice young woman who loves her children, and finds her role as wife and mother quite fulfilling. But that she finds this disciplinary measure an acceptable one is interesting. In some ways, Janet measures up pretty well to at least one or two aspects of what makes a good disciplinarian. She doesn't make threats, and she is consistent. She merely demonstrated to the children what she would do if they didn't do as they were told, and then followed through until they thoroughly understood and behaved accordingly.

I have never battered or willfully neglected one of my children and I cannot imagine a circumstance that would lead to a premeditated spread-eagle job. But on more than one occasion when one of them has misbehaved, I have been so enraged that instead of hitting a child, I have slammed my fist into a wall, or bolted from the house. Once I have calmed down I have reflected on two things:

146

that my rage was almost never in proportion to the seriousness of what my child had done; and, more significant, I have always wondered what stopped me dead in my tracks in the middle of trembling anger—from beating.

Rita, according to an article on child-battering in *Family Health* magazine,[4] is a pretty, composed young suburban housewife with three children. One of her children is a beautiful four-year-old girl who is "the image of her mother." This little girl was recently hospitalized after her mother pushed her down a flight of stairs—one in a string of similar incidents. Her mother is terrified of what she will do when her child is sent home. Hard as it may be to understand, Rita loves her child and wants her safe from harm. This mother recognizes that she represents a threat to her child's safety. Why does this nice middle-class woman beat her little girl?

Rita herself was a battered child—and she is a battering mother who abuses the only one of her three children who bears a physical resemblance to her.

Another mother, Mrs. K., described in an article by Dr. Vincent Fontana in *Medical Insight*,[5] has this to say: "I was . . . appalled to discover . . . I had spells of unprovoked viciousness toward my child. With the craftiness of a sick mind I hid all evidence of scars or bruises, or lied to explain them away. But something rational still operated enough to insist that my behavior was highly abnormal, and that I needed help. The horrible thing was that I did not know where to go for help, and even when I finally forced myself to the offices of various social agencies, I was so afraid of having the child taken away and my behavior thus exposed to friends and relatives that I could hardly speak of the problem. Even when I could, I found that social workers could not really help me. . . . Finally I moved up through the bureaus and agencies to a psychiatrist. Here I obtained help, but I might add that many people could not afford this."

In her letter, this mother went on to say that she herself had been battered by her stepfather.

In a study of sixty families with battered children,

University of Colorado psychiatrists Brand F. Steele and Carl B. Pollock discovered only one characteristic all the parents had in common. As children they had been battered themselves, either physically or emotionally: "All had experienced a sense of intense, pervasive, continuous demand from their parents. A sense of constant parental criticism. No matter what the patient as a child tried to do, it was not enough, it was not right, it was at the wrong time, it bothered the parents, it would disgrace the parents in the eyes of the world."

The pattern repeats itself when these children grow up and have children of their own. Overdisciplined and deprived of parental love in their infancy, they look to their own children for what they missed. "Axiomatic to the child beater," say Pollock and Steele, "are that infants' needs are unimportant and should be disregarded, and that children who do not fulfill these requirements deserve punishment." [6]

According to Inspector Mel Leathley of the San Francisco Juvenile Bureau, battering parents are from absolutely every socio-economic group. He feels that many cases go unreported: "Battering shows up on court records more among poor families because the poor usually take their children to county hospitals, which report the cases. Battered middle-class and upper-middle-class children are usually taken to private physicians, many of whom don't report the offense."

In defining the potential child abusers, Carol Schneider, Carl Pollock, and Ray E. Helfer say this in *Helping the Battered Child and His Family:* [7]

Parents who physically abuse their small children have, almost invariably, been reared in a similar manner. At least the relationship they had as small children with their own parents left a great deal to be desired. They truly were never or poorly "imprinted" with that highly important and essential ability to "mother" a small child.

Research into the problem of child abuse is certainly

warranted. But, as we look back at our own childhoods, how many of us can say with certainty that the relationship we had with our parents did not leave a great deal to be desired. How many of us can say we were "imprinted" with that "highly important and essential ability to 'mother' a small child"? Defined in that way, it would seem that a large segment of the American public can be said to be "potential" child abusers. And perhaps it is.

9
Marital bliss and children

There are two marriages in every marital union, his and hers, and his is better than hers.

—JESSIE BERNARD

WHEN I WAS FIVE MONTHS PREGNANT with my first child, my husband and I celebrated our eighth wedding anniversary. He gave me an exquisite bracelet, made of thousands of tiny seed pearls. It was elegant, feminine, and provocative—everything he believed me to be.

Six years later, I was picking up the pearls in my vacuum cleaner and by hand whenever I spotted one on the floor. That torn and twisted bracelet is a sad symbol of the effect two children have had on a once beautiful relationship. My young and very beloved son destroyed that token of my husband's devotion, and to some extent the affection and devotion itself slipped away in the complicated and demanding process of caring for small children.

I didn't have to read most of the popular ladies' magazines to know that children add a new dimension to marriage. I found it out by becoming a mother, and I also learned that the dimension added is not quite what *Redbook, Good Housekeeping. The Ladies' Home Journal,* and all the other publications that tell women their marriages can be either enhanced or saved by having children make it out to be.

In her statement presented to the Senate Labor and Public Welfare Committee, Ellen Peck, author of *The Baby Trap,* posed the question: "*Does* Baby save marriage?" She then went on: "To find a realistic answer, it's necessary to leave the *Ladies' Home Journal* and go to the professional journals." [1]

Dr. E. E. LeMasters reports in an article in *Marriages and Family Living* titled "Parenthood as Crises," that extensive or severe home crisis situations occurred following the birth of a child in 83 percent of the cases he studied.[2] Arthur P. Jacoby tells us that 87 percent of new parents were disturbed rather than pleased with the changed family situation.[3] Dr. Harold Feldman, a professor in the Department of Human Development and Family Studies at Cornell University, says that in a study of 852 middle-class and upper-class urban couples, "those with children had a significant lower level of marital satisfaction than those without children. When a couple become parents the marital satisfaction declines." [4]

In summing up the findings of Dr. Feldman, Anna and Arnold Silverman in *The Case Against Having Children* postulate, "The reasons for the decline in marital satisfaction are largely the same as those which caused the initial adjustment crises following the birth of their first child. We can assume then that the psychologically, physically, and socially unsatisfactory conditions of early parenthood did not disappear as adjustment took place but rather that they became an integral part of the family relationship." [5]

The seeds of discord between a married couple with children, according to Dr. LeMasters, are sown just shortly after the birth of a child. There are studies that can pin dissatisfaction or stress down to nocturnal feedings, loss of sleep, dirty diapers, loss of freedom, financial demands, or the combination. There are studies enough to make you fall asleep from dry statistics and tedious psychology, dealing, for example, with the loss of sleep of new parents, so why belabor the obvious? No one really likes to be awakened in the middle of the night by a crying baby or relishes changing dirty diapers.

It is common for ill-prepared new parents to be not quite so pleased as they had anticipated about the whole scene. And if a little innocent baby who hasn't even learned how to run the television set full blast yet can be a cause for "severe home crises" it ought not be too difficult to accept that a growing child can wreak havoc in a marriage. For a lot of parents coping with real children doing real things is more disturbing than the upheaval a baby causes by simply getting born.

For those who have not experienced, first hand, the realities of rearing young children and trying to make a marriage work, these statistics and conclusions may come as a revelation. However, those of us who *have* experienced it can skip the professional journals, and find realistic answers to Ms. Peck's question without ever leaving the kitchen.

One evening my husband and I had a blockbuster over shredded potatoes. It was nearly divorce after that episode. My hostility level was *unbelievable* (until recent years, I have been known for my great patience). My husband, normally a quiet, sensitive man, displayed sheer hatred. Another time, I (Shirley, the Pacifist) threw an egg across the kitchen in the middle of a discussion that had nothing to do with our personal lives. When the smoke cleared, we were astonished to find out that we had not even been in disagreement.

Just before both of these idiotic demonstrations, a variation on the following theme was taking place: I was preparing dinner, the TV set was blaring, the kids were wrestling on the floor, screaming at the top of their lungs, one or the other of them had kicked over a glass of milk (which one or the other of them had put on the floor), and my husband had just walked wearily into the kitchen, stepping on raisins and Rice Krispies along the way.

In a similar setting, a friend of mine who rarely raises her voice threw a hamburger at her husband; he stalked out of the house, leaving one of his business cards on her pillow. Another generally nonviolent woman cleared the drainboard off in fifteen seconds flat—onto the floor—when her husband commented on the messy kitchen at just the wrong moment.

Disproportionate rage is common in homes where young children generate almost constant confusion, noise, and messes. The fuse can get very short, very fast, and a trivial incident can trigger an ugly and sometimes a dangerous, dispute. Women aren't exactly eager to admit to this sort of behavior, and yet most of the women I spoke to had had more than a taste or two of it.

These blowups in any marriage are just the tip of the iceberg. There is a complicated undercurrent operating most of the time—pervasive resentment that, even without whopping battles, can turn a happy marriage into a shambles. Equality in marriage makes very good sense, if only because it is a fair way to proceed. But egalitarian marriages are not the rule, nor are homes with servants to relieve the mother of all the trivia of housekeeping. (And relief from the trivia of housekeeping is scarcely an all-purpose answer.) Nor are women who hold satisfying jobs outside the home and who have managed to escape in large measure the attendant guilt the rule. A combination of the above could, perhaps, be put forth as an ideal situation in which children might not affect the happiness of the marriage. But this set of circumstances is rare. And even where it is found, those mothers still feel that their marriage would be more solid had they no children. For the sake of this discussion, the focal point will be middle-class housewives who, like myself, are part of The Great American Dream and who, by the precepts of that dream, spend the majority of our days as wives and mothers.

Since Betty Friedan wrote *The Feminine Mystique* nearly a decade ago, women may be more aware of the myths surrounding motherhood but, for all the punch and validity of that important book, most of its readers said, "yes, yes," and then went ahead and did the expected thing. We got married and we had kids, and we tried all the new floor waxes and laundry detergents, baked bread, and made our own clothes. The here and now for most women has not changed one hell of a lot.

We may be in the throes of a serious revolution, but right now the situation is that the average middle-class couple with kids reflects the good old American traditional concept that says parenthood is fulfilling, and that having children is part of a happy and fulfilling marriage. But for many women, the traditional values fall flat.

Those who would challenge the argument that the concerns and tensions of motherhood and the medium of homemaking add up to a difficult and unpleasant task would probably admit that many women do find it difficult and unpleasant and resent the demands that are placed on them. They may, quite simply, not like the job they're handed.

People in unpleasant employment situations are not happy people, and frequently they find themselves resenting their employers. A wife who sees herself stuck with all the crappy jobs may resent her husband for making her a mother. Most women who, when childless, never really minded much when their husbands read the newspaper while they took care of traditionally wifely chores become resentful, if not downright angry when simultaneously correcting young children, cleaning up their spills, and soothing their hurts is added. While the Lord of the Manor, seemingly removed from the situation, is sipping a cocktail, listening to Bach, and reading the Dow-Jones averages, a seething resentment builds that can lead to a dispute he in no way expects ("What's all this confusion got to do with *me?*") Sometimes, of course, a mother/wife just tucks this new irritation away in her "hostility compartment" as part of a growing collection. The undercurrent of hostility is kept building.

What changes once-gentle tolerance or mild annoyance toward a husband who does little more than sit around into outright hostility is, most usually, children. It is the children who put the woman on twenty-four-hour call, who make her job harder. It is the children who snap the trap shut and cause the woman to gravitate to the role that ties her to the home. She feels that she *must.* And all the abstracts and theories of women's liberation cannot change the feelings of most mothers.

Several things add to the resentment that many women feel about holding down a job they don't like and resenting their husbands for forcing them into that job. Just as it is still the responsibility of the woman to care for home and children, whenever anyone talks about "making marriage work," the onus for bringing off the operation is put on the female partner. The same magazines that carry stories on how baby saves marriage are full of articles with titles like, "How to Hold Your Man," "How to Make Your Marriage Exciting," "How to Keep Him from Straying."

Besides the unfairness of the idea that one party of a marriage should be responsible for the success or failure of the relationship, and the attendant resentment that unfairness may cause, there is a small degree of blackmail involved that hardly causes warm feelings. If never explicitly stated, the message is: Keep him happy if you want to stay married. Blackmail can exist only if there is need, and need—for most women—is caused by their children. Being a mother takes away for most women (for all practical and relatively unpainful purposes) the option of not being married. The unpleasant paradox is that the children who are so much at the root of the conflict between husband and wife are almost always the consideration that traps a woman into a marriage she might well wish to be out of. That divorce for many women is scarcely a welcome and viable option (what will it do to the kids?) can make a woman all the more resentful. And what of the father who has bought the same bill of goods as the mother? True, he is not subject to the intense feelings of responsibility, guilt, and fear that his wife is. (Although, certainly, he is subject to some and those feelings may make him a less than happy person.) Yet why, he may justifiably wonder, can't she make him a home and family the way it's supposed to be. It is a rare husband who doesn't feel cheated and resentful of his wife's resentment. It is a vicious circle and in the middle of the circle sit the children.

A marriage that can withstand the trials of children— surviving in feeling as well as name—is a rare one. A woman who dislikes her role and responsibilities as a mother may be quite unhappy, and there cannot exist a happy marriage where one of the partners is unhappy. As

157

one woman very pointedly put it, "My husband is a very happily married man—I'm miserable. Our marriage is a dismal failure."

Marriage, for all its own and very special joys, is not without its problems. Two people who spend their lives together are bound to have differences and difficulties. Yet, after children come, differences and difficulties multiply in most marriages and most of those differences and difficulties are directly or indirectly traceable to those children.

One woman said that a common battle she and her husband had early in marriage resulted from her rather casual approach to housework, and his fastidiousness.

We were able to resolve this in the early days of marriage because it's a lot easier to be an artful and careful homemaker when you don't have kids. After the kids came, it became increasingly difficult. Not so much when they were very small, but as they grew it became a real contest to keep things in good shape. We went from a well-maintained home, good meals, order, and a pleasant, well-groomed wife to a real shambles—with me trying to keep up the standards we, particularly my husband, had grown accustomed to.

Imagine for a moment the feelings of a forty-year-old man who has become accustomed to a particularly pleasant and desirable life style. He enters his home each night, not to the sights and sounds he has enjoyed for a number of years, but instead to the sights of total disorder and the sounds of crisis (Johnny just fell out of the tree), a distraught, nervous wife, dinner half started, perhaps half burned, food on the floor that gets stuck to his shoes, house half cleaned, and the TV going full blast.

What's noteworthy is her conclusion:

Imagine, also, my own frustration, when I've knocked myself out all day trying to maintain a nice home and been frustrated by my children and their playmates at every turn. The kids vomiting, breaking things, crying, falling out of trees, bumping heads, skinning knees, getting into mischief—these things mess up the simplest plans. While I love the children dearly, I can't help resenting my husband's lack of understanding, and I wind up resenting everyone and everything and, as usual, feeling incredibly guilty. It's hard to blame the kids, but you really have to admit that if it weren't for them, the reason for this tense situation wouldn't exist.

It's all too easy to argue that women shouldn't be so concerned with the state of their homes or with pleasing their husbands. Yet the reality exists and reality is what we are exploring.

Another young woman, shocked by the realities of parenthood but more capable of saying, "Oh, well, what the hell" said that in the early days, she really did feel bad and guilty, of all things, when her husband came through the door expecting her to be all pretty and the house to be looking lovely, only to find a stack of unfolded diapers on the sofa and his wife with her hair still in rollers. She said, "He didn't have to say a word, one look at his face conveyed precisely his disappointment—the acknowledgment that the honeymoon was indeed over.

There are more stories of women who have truly tried to be first-rate homemakers and have been frustrated in the process because of the demands made by their young children. We could talk at length about how they feel about their husbands, their children, their marriages, and their self-worth. But it seems enough to say that so many of us try so hard to bring off the world's greatest domestic scene, only to know failure. It hurts—first not to make the grade, and then it hurts more to know we've knocked ourselves out and no one really notices or seems to care.

My husband feels that a well-ordered world is little to ask and that it should always be a fact of life. And I can't say that I blame him for feeling that way. He works hard all day and what does he come home to? He has little understanding of what is involved in the day-to-day routine, and for all I know he thinks that Samantha the Witch runs around in his house all day. He seems vaguely amazed when I have to do more than twitch my nose to keep everything in apple-pie order. I used to be very frustrated because I couldn't quite win the gold star in homemaking—somehow the little kids not only got in the way of this dubious achievement while I was trying to get it all together during the day, but it continued well into the evening. Most of the time I was able to bring off the beautiful setting, but the ultimate goal of having everything in good shape by 6 o'clock, and having that be the end of the matter, just isn't a real one the way it was before we had children. It didn't take me long to realize that a woman can spend the entire day working and not be at all off the hook at day's end. For young children, there are baths, stories to be read, questions to be answered, getting them into pajamas, brushing their teeth, picking up toys, putting things away, and when they're older teaching them how to, and after that making sure they do it.

When my husband comes home at night and has the audacity to tell me how tired he is, I'm either obviously annoyed or stick that comment where it adds to the others to come out later and worse. Either attitude doesn't do our relationship much good. So he's tired, is he? Well, I'm still hard at it, and as he mixes the drinks and flakes out on the sofa with the newspaper or a good book, I always think rather angrily of the old proverb: "A man may work from sun to sun—a woman's work is never done," and I get doubly mad because I am, after all, a twentieth-century woman. Sometimes while these crucial thoughts are occupying what once was my mind, I note, as I zigzag through the house performing the endless routine, that instead of reading, he is listening to a new record—a record I can never quite hear during this period because the kitchen is on the other side of the house.

I remember one time after my husband told me how tired he was and settled in with his drink and newspaper, I joined him in the living room for my usual ten minutes of maintaining the illusion of "you're home now, how nice to see you, let's make believe nothing much has changed from the pre-kid days." Probably just to make conversation he said, "Gee, you've got spots on that nice dress."

"SPOTS!" I spat. "Look at the scars on my arms and hands from *cooking!* Cooking with little children underfoot. Let me tell you how many times I've been so distracted and my mind so jumbled that I picked up a casserole dish without using pot holders. *And* how about the time I nearly took off my index finger with an electric knife? SPOTS??? You'd have spots, yes even you, if you had to be a drudge. In fact the spots won't even come out of this dress, and that really makes me uptight, because I don't have many dresses. By the way, that reminds me, I ironed today. Did you know that you have twenty-seven shirts? Excuse me, I *must* finish cooking dinner."

I'm not terribly proud of behavior like that. When I realize that I've hurt some feelings or been insensitive to things that might be troubling my husband, I feel bad and know that he scarcely deserves such treatment. But this is the kind of thinking, or non-thinking, that is behind such an outburst. Here I've been cooped up with the kids, the dog, the stove, and the termite man all day, and I've somehow struggled through sufficiently to have dinner well on its way and enough of the routine taken care of as possible, and I've put on the only decent clean dress —spots and all—I have in an effort to look halfway presentable. Then he walks through the door and in five minutes, he's telling me how tired *he* is, followed by how much the kids get on *his* nerves, and soon after that discussing the spots on my dress. FIVE MINUTES OF THE KIDS AND HIS PRECIOUS NERVES ARE SHOT! What in the hell does he think *mine* must be like? That is, of course, if he ever thinks about *my* nerves, and at this point of conflict that too is always doubtful.

"I have the feeling," said one friend, "that if I dropped dead on the spot, my husband would be *annoyed*. Not grief-stricken, but annoyed because he's tired and my demise would be just one more inconvenience."

It is very difficult for many women to admit, even to themselves, that they resent their children and feel trapped because of their motherhood. Their children, they feel, are innocent. Certainly not all mothers are this benevolent, but one mother speaks for many on this aspect of the effects of young children on marriage: "I was most reluctant to admit, even to myself, that my longed-for, planned, and terribly wonderful children could be resented even mildly—because, by God, they didn't ask to be born and I owe it to them to give them every benefit of the best I have to offer as their mother. I did realize at some point, after considerable damage had been done to our marriage, that a lot of the anger I was directing toward my husband was quite misplaced. I was angry at the children because they were more troublesome than I ever imagined that children might be, but because it isn't 'normal' to have these feelings about little beloved innocents, the target for my wrath wound up being the male adult who turned me into a mother. To admit this is not in any way painless."

The story of women resenting their husbands because they appear the best people to blame for dreariness is not a new one. One woman I know has detested her husband since their son was two years old. They have two children, and since the birth of their second child two years after the first, their domestic situation deteriorated steadily. The woman is a very talented musician, but she and her husband could never afford any household help or even an occasional babysitter; developing, or even enjoying, her talent and years of training was a nearly insurmountable task while the kids were little. Every scale and every note practiced was the result of rigid and careful planning, eking out a half hour here and there, often only to be interrupted by the needs of her small children. She became very bitter and showed her resentment of her husband in many ways, the least destructive in her often-uttered cliché "If it weren't for him . . ."

While this woman was, and is, an excellent mother, her marriage became a shambles. The things that kept her from fulfilling herself as an individual and thus led to her becoming extremely hostile had little at all to do with her husband, except that he couldn't afford to provide her with time of her own. Yet, if this couple hadn't had children, would she have any reasons for being bitter? It's interesting that despite all the bitterness over the years, now that their kids are in college their relationship is improving.

Another woman had this to say: "I don't know him any more. Before Tommy was born, I thought he was the kindest and most considerate man in the world. It's shocking to see how uninterested he is in our child and how little interest he has these days in my pursuits and problems. He has no understanding of the difficulties there are in raising a child, and yet when we had no children, he was always so very considerate of me. During those days, after I got off work, he was the one to say, "Take it easy, honey, you've put in a hard day." And now, he won't even watch the child willingly so that I can enjoy a minute off now and again."

Molly, the mother of four girls, traces the root of her marital disharmony to the fact that her husband takes her for granted, but never takes her any place. They no longer visit their friends without taking the kids along because they have nowhere to leave them, and similarly they no longer have their friends in for an evening's entertainment because "there are too many demands generated by the kids." Who, really, is keeping her from enjoying life as she would like. Her husband? Her kids? In her view, her husband is the villain, but she rarely says anything to him about it. Telling another woman may give vent to some hostility but it certainly doesn't make it disappear. It merely serves to reinforce her conviction that her husband keeps her from having a happy life and helps her to ignore the fact that they were quite happy before the kids came along. In fact, they were very much in love and enjoyed their life together before they had children, just as most of us do who get married in the first place. It certainly isn't mutual hatred that brings us together.

The feelings of so many mothers seem well put by one mother of three: "As soon as I hear the crunch of Jim's tires in our gravel driveway each evening, I'm automatically irritated."

It is interesting to look at marriages, totally successful for many years, that have undergone radical changes since children were born.

Helen and Jack were married for seven years before they had children. We spent many weekends with them (we were childless for a bit longer than they), and it was so obvious that they had a magnificent relationship. One rarely sees a couple who are lovers and friends, and who even possess the ability to work well together. But these two worked side by side for years and seemed to enjoy every minute of it. In the early years, when Jack was going to school, we used to count pennies to see if we could go out and have a pitcher of beer together. Today, they can afford a trip to Europe and a beautiful home; Helen no longer has to think twice about buying a new dress. And today, they have one son and they are barely on speaking terms.

After they had been married for seven years, Helen gave birth to a lovely baby and she did everything just right. Natural childbirth, rooming in; she breast-fed that baby until he was eight months old. She is, to this day, one of the most loving, tender mothers imaginable. But then Helen is a very loving kind woman. She loves her son, but she does admit freely that another child would do her in and that her very cherished little boy drives her nuts.

The first hint that something was wrong came one day when I dropped by her house for a quick cup of coffee. Everything was fine, except that she didn't know if Jack was coming home for dinner; she went on to say that she never knew any more when he might be home any night before midnight. I found it difficult, in my naïveté (I was pregnant with my first child) to believe that their unity was not even further cemented now that they had Alan.

After seven beautiful years, the joy of motherhood was not a bonus to Helen's already quite lovely life. A very nice marriage was the price she paid for her motherhood.

Jack tried hard, in his own way, to be a good husband and father, but he had difficulty accepting the fact that he had to share his wife, or worse yet, take a back seat. The child's noise and crying bothered him, and as the boy got older, the messes he made drove his father nearly mad. Helen became quite defensive about everything that Jack found objectionable. He would be firm with their son, and she would think him unreasonable and tell him as much. She would be loving and kind, and he'd feel shut out. Both Helen and Jack wanted to be good parents: They simply had different ideas about rearing children. These differences gave way to a display of qualities to each other that never would have surfaced had they remained childless.

Friends and acquaintances became witnesses to their snide remarks to and about each other, their outright battles and tears of agony as time went on. Two discreet people who had shown the utmost respect for each other were now *fighting in public!* Helen is fighting to hold her marriage together—a marriage that was built on all of the right premises, and was so solid that for seven years neither partner had to work, let alone fight, to maintain it.

Helen's situation doesn't really have much to do with a wife becoming a mother and therefore becoming dowdy, dull, or sexless. It more realistically underscores the responsibilities and agonies of parenthood. Helen's story is not unique. It is much like many others that show a change in a basically good relationship after the children come on the scene—changes that occur when hitherto unknown qualities of both parties emerge because of parenthood, and when a life style has been radically and irreversibly changed.

Joanne and Joe were married for fifteen years before they had their first child. They appeared to have an idyllic marriage; like Helen and Jack once were, they were friends and lovers. The one acknowledged flaw in their marriage was that they had no children. Joanne learned that surgery could correct her infertility, and she was grateful. The operation was successful, and they had

165

two children, a boy and a girl. They were absolutely delighted—for a while. After their little boy passed the magic age of three, and their little girl started making noises like a real child, it didn't take long for Joan to experience all the joys and realities of parenthood and discover that it wasn't quite what she had expected it to be. And Joanne was in for a few surprises about her husband.

Where once, all these years, she thought Joe was the finest man she knew, she discovered that he had some unpalatable ideas about raising a son. Joe liked to hunt. He was disappointed when he learned that his six-year-old son could not bear to see an animal killed. He tried to make a man of him, and succeeded in making him stutter. He had his own methods of dealing with the stuttering, too, and all the while Joanne got more frantic.

While Joe's behavior can hardly be condoned, had this couple never had children this unreasonable trait would not have shown itself. But this, and apparently some other qualities, emerged because on more than one occasion Joanne indicated that unless Joe changed appreciably, she would take the children and leave. LEAVE! For fifteen years this couple was happy together and deeply in love. Now that she has children—or rather now that *they* have children—*she is talking about leaving.*

It seems only fair to discuss the man's point of view. A man's happiness certainly has a good deal to do with the success of a marriage. It can't be comfortable to live with the financial responsibility for three or four other people, to be constantly concerned that the bed and board for his family is dependent upon him. Many men become locked into jobs they detest because they need the financial security—something they probably would not need so much if they were not fathers.

Yet it is hard for a mother to sympathize fully with her husband. In *The Baby Trap,* Ellen Peck quotes *Baltimore Sun* writer R. H. Gardner when he asks, "How many young men's dreams have been sacrificed to the need of a modern kitchen, separate bedrooms for the children,

166

and an education at the college of their choice?" I read that to one woman who applied it to her husband, her life, and her family life with him. Her response was at first sympathetic, but then, after thinking it over for a moment, she went on.

What, in God's name, about my dreams? My husband may have sacrificed some of his dreams because he has kids, but he didn't trade serenity for a *nightmare* that goes on every single day. What about my dreams? A *woman* has no dreams?

What about even a little dream? The big ones have been relegated to a back shelf somewhere in our minds. But even working in an office every day and not having the total responsibility for children's baths, dinners, laundry, going through the chaos and confusion, the knee-weakening situations, and all of the other tedious chores shoved at the marriage partner who stays home —even working in a dull office can look like *paradise.* Don't give me any garbage about *his* dreams and expect me to feel sad. So the old boy can't sail a skiff around the world, work in causes, or while away his days with a paint box; at least he's not further insulted by being confined to four walls every day doing janitorial service. So the guy's job at Zilch Corporation isn't the most exciting one in the world—mine is??? Do you think that most women wouldn't trade places with their husbands, just like that? Do you think that men would trade places with their wives?

To a shut-in like me, my husband's life looks absolutely dazzling. He's not a movie producer or an airline pilot; he's just an average working guy like millions of others. *But*—he gets up every morning, puts on some clothes that someone else laundered for him eats breakfast that someone else prepared for him, gives his children a fond pat on their little heads, kisses his wife, and leaves for the office. *Leaves!* He doesn't even have to make arrangements for a babysitter or leave instructions. He already has a permanent babysitter, working for a very low wage, and she is completely familiar with the children, their needs, and the household chores. He gets in his car and he drives to work. He enters the building and says a cheery hello to the pretty receptionist, proceeds to his office, and performs some tasks that he enjoys. Yes he enjoys his work. He takes coffee breaks, he has lunch hours, and occasionally he goes out with his friends for cocktails and lunch. He does some more work, and then he drives home, stopping along the way at the record store or maybe the book store, or drops by the shopping center for a loaf of bread and discovers that there is an art show in progress. He spends some time there and then he comes home. He mixes drinks and says, "Hey, did you know that Phil Futz and old Ethel are getting married?" Let me tell you about a new artist—I went to this art show while I was picking up the bread. How was your day?" "Oh yes, very interesting about the termite man." To say that I'm jealous of his freedom is an understatement. A few years back a survey indicated that when it came to wives being jealous of their husbands, the vast majority of women said they most envied their husbands' freedom—their ability to more or less come and go at will. Before we had children, I had no such feelings, because I too could leave the house without taking along my constant companions or making arrangements for their care. I also had a car. I also had a very interesting job. And my own money.

"But the other side of that," explained my husband "is, that however right or wrong my perceptions are, I feel that I *must* get up at a fixed time, *must* put on the suit and tie, and *must* be somewhere every day at a fixed hour. While it's good that you get up early to see to the children and see everyone off, you don't really *have* to. The children are old enough to get themselves dressed and grab a bowl of cereal, and I certainly don't need you to take care of my dressing and breakfasting. You *could* sleep as late as you like, and you don't have to get dressed and go somewhere every day. Your time is really your own, even though you don't see it that way. You don't, for example, go to an office every day to bring home the money for the very food we all eat—and you don't worry about things like whether your life insurance would be sufficient to take care of the family, as you watch men my age dropping dead from heart attacks."

He's right—to a degree. But the reasons that his perceptions are wrong are that first, I'm a responsible person, and second, I believe that if I sat around and ate bonbons all day, didn't see the kids off, and didn't take my obligations seriously, whatever feeling he has for me would turn into sheer hatred and contempt, and he probably wouldn't stay around.

We are told by many experts that husbands often feel left out after their wives have babies. The love of his life no longer showers him with the attention he has become accustomed to receiving. And very often his once-beautiful lover turns into someone's rather unglamorous mother —this can be most disappointing.

It is at this point, we are warned by the ladies' magazines and other experts, that he might start looking at the girls in the office and his friends' better-kempt wives, and make some unflattering comparisons. He may even be thinking that in addition to his wife becoming dowdy, she's becoming a bit of a bore. So maybe he starts thinking about doing a little more than just looking—now that the old girl is not looking so well, no longer the bright, witty, leggy life of the party. Well, dammit, what about *her?* Don't her feelings and disappointments count for anything? Somehow it's accepted that men stray and quit loving their wives after motherhood does its unglamorous tricks. Did you ever notice how many middle-aged men trade in their worn-out wives for newer, younger models —the wives they wore out by keeping them pregnant and barefoot and chained to the stove?

As one man put it, "I love my wife, or rather, I used to before we had kids and she changed." Why did she change? How do you think she feels? Some women just feel bad—they get hurt when they learn that the man they love can be so superficial, and that the woman who's tried to make him happy can't offer him nearly as much as the pretty secretary who has joined the firm.

For some women the effect is interesting. They begin

not to care if their husbands start looking around. As one woman said, "I wish to God he *would* get a girl friend— then maybe he'd leave me alone. I simply can't stand him any more."

And there's another side of the coin. "There's a type of man," said a friend, "who, after he's made his wife pregnant and turned her into a domestic slave, then has the gall to blame her because the marriage is no longer *exciting*. Speaking to such a man, I'd say this: Don't forget —the iceman cometh, and *his* wife may be even uglier."

The same man who would acknowledge that if his wife is uninterested in him or if he loses interest in her, it's perfectly all right and acceptable for him to look else-where for exciting feminine companionship, would find it unacceptable for his wife to do the same thing. Many men don't recognize that women have the same needs, and an uninteresting or uninterested husband can drive a woman to have affairs.

Margaret said:

I was convinced that it was love. But looking back, I think I was a little crazy at the time. The kids were driving me mad, my husband, Dick, seemed to regard me with disgust most of the time—he was annoyed by my attitude toward the children, couldn't under-stand how I could possibly be so nervous, and he started turning away from me more and more. I know you'll find this hard to believe, but our relationship deterior-ated to such an extent that at one point he didn't lay a hand on me for six months. When I tried to reach out to him, he simply turned his back on me. I'm a healthy and loving woman, and celibacy is simply not my bag. This left me wide open for the first man who came along, and unfortunately, because of the con-ditioning put on *my* generation, you've simply got to be in love to go to bed with someone.

Anyway, there was a young man in Dick's office. He wasn't married, so Dick frequently invited him over. He encouraged me to invite him to parties at our house, and to dig up girls for him. He seemed to be a really sweet guy, and attractive in his own way. He complimented me on my cooking, the way my hair looked, and once in a while I thought I saw him casting meaningful glances in my direction. One day, after the kids left for school, Lou—that was his name—surprised me with a phone call. He said he had a problem, and having few friends in the area, felt the need to talk, so naturally he thought of me, what with us being such good friends and all. He asked me to have lunch with him. To this day, I can't remember what his problem was, or what we talked about over chilled wine and oysters Rockefeller, but that was the beginning of the end for me. The next time (oh, yes there were many next times) he called, he said that he had taken a day off from work and he wanted my advice on decorating his apartment—ho, ho. By this time, I was fascinated by the man, and of course I was feeling a good bit of hostility toward my husband. I went over to his apartment and made a few suggestions, but he wasn't all that interested in homemaking. At first I struggled. Struggled with him, and then myself, and then said, "Oh, what the hell," and ultimately wound up having a dumb affair that lasted for two years. All the while it was going on I was convinced I was in love, and if I was crazy when I started the thing, it was nothing compared to the insanity of two years of pretending we were just good friends with Dick bringing him home from the office a couple of evenings each week. By day, when Lou could get away from the office, we were lovers; by night, with Dick around, Lou was just a friend of the family.

Lou finally found a "nice girl" and got married, and of course we're just a wholesome foursome now. Every time they come over to the house or invite us to their place, it's excruciating. I have to keep up a good front, so I'll play along and suffer in silence, hating both Lou and Dick. Lou for enjoying this little farce, and Dick for rejecting me and making me vulnerable. And I know that if I hadn't been so wrapped up in the kids, Dick wouldn't have turned away.

Even without infidelity on either side thrown in, the strains caused by a change in life style, the resentments of the wife, the resentments of the husband make a far from rosy situation.

That kids can cause specific disputes is just one more burden on an already strained relationship. And children do indeed cause parents to argue with each other. Sometimes it is innocent and unintentional, born out of a difference of opinion about child-rearing. Sometimes the kids quite intentionally pit one parent against the other—to gain attention, to get permission to do something or go somewhere, or just to see if they can bring it off. As one teacher put it, "Kids have real ESP; they know exactly what's going on; they're more clever than we believe."

The most obvious and commonly staged battle occurs when a child wants something he is not sure he can have. He will ask one parent for whatever it is, and if that parent says no, he will wait a decent interval and ask the other. Until my husband and I became more experienced one of us would fall into this trap, and then we'd have the usual arguments about undermining someone else's authority. And usually the entire matter was over nothing more important than a cookie.

The parents of a little boy I'll call Timmy have a basic difference of opinion over how to handle their child. When Timmy's father disciplines him, he almost always runs sobbing to his mother for comfort. Sometimes, not knowing what's happened, she innocently comforts her hurt child. Sometimes she has known about and disagreed with the action and ends up simultaneously comforting the child and scolding her husband. The child now knows that Mom will probably come to the rescue, and he takes full advantage of it. According to Dr. Spock, letting a child cause this sort of dissension can be psychologically damaging *to the child*. But parents find it difficult always to present a unified front, especially when they privately disagree. Timmy, through this ploy, has managed to drive a wedge between his parents—an accomplishment, Dr. Spock adds ironically, that can cause a kind of guilt in young children with which they're not equipped to cope. The paradox is quite pretty. We must not let the children

172

affect a marriage adversely because it is upsetting to the children.

With all of the staged battles, the actual blowups, the differences of opinion regarding the kids, the undercurrent of negative feelings each partner may have about his or her respective responsibilities and role, the confusion, work, worry, and chaos—a once happily married couple can become so sensitized that even trivial irritations or imagined slights can take on exaggerated proportions.

Maybe a wife "hasn't had time" to talk to him about something or other because she has been busy with the children or busy preparing dinner. Then the phone rings; it's the friend not heard from for some time, and suddenly she has time to chat for a few minutes. Then the kids start acting up while she's talking (they always do when the phone rings) and she calls in to him to "*do* something," perhaps with a note of irritation in her voice—returning to the call on a brisk cheery note ("somehow she can always be nice to *other* people") Or she doesn't have time to sew a button on his shirt, but he comes home and finds her playing Scrabble with one of the kids. Or they have just spent part of the evening in stony silence and friends drop in unexpectedly, and she's suddenly the life of the party. Or he's in the middle of paying the bills, and he's trying to trace an error in the checkbook; she's in the kitchen, clearing up the dishes, the kids are acting up, and it's time for their baths, and she interrupts him at a crucial moment of accounting, imploring him to "at least assume *part* of your responsibility, and help with the kids."

Forty percent of all marriages in America end in divorce, and since children are an integral part of marriage in our culture, it is a safe bet that the vast majority of couples who terminate their marriages have at least one child. In the July, 1972, issue of *Family Health,* Jack Harrison Pollack reports that growing numbers of couples seeking divorce are couples whose children have grown and left the nest.[6] The reason most frequently given for ending these long marriages is "we only stayed together because of the children—now that they are grown, we can get the divorce we've wanted for many years." If these late divorces are indeed becoming more prevalent, then the obvious question is, how many husbands and wives who are presently living together and raising their children—looking all the while as if they are genuinely compatible—will divorce after the children, who probably caused the havoc in these once good relationships, are grown? And take a good look around at all the couples you know who have gotten a divorce. Fine. Now, how many of them were childless couples? How many were childless couples who were married for over five years?

It would be foolish to suggest that childless couples are consistently serene, that they never have squabbles—or even downright good battles—because, unless it's a union of vegetables, there are bound to be disagreements between two people who live together. But it is considerably easier to get back on good footing with each other if the relationship has not been bombarded with confusion and chaos, and each partner's own dissatisfactions. Making up after a tiff can be a lot of fun—and very sweet. One wonders how many battle-scarred couples with children even bother to make up any more.

The marriage that is *enhanced* by children is truly rare; the marriage that remains intact a monumental achievement. Many marriages deteriorate simply because there are so many forces at work, any one of which, by itself, could destroy a marriage. Once children become part of the delicate relationship between a man and a woman, the same couple that loved each other enough to make a long-term commitment and have pulled together as a devoted unit starts pulling apart, and starts being pulled apart by all of the new problems, worries, and inner conflicts.

What brings a couple together in the beginning becomes forgotten in the process of struggling to raise a family. Sometimes, when we become nostalgic about this loss, we are accused of being hopeless romantics. We are urged to grow up, to assume our responsibilities. It is as if society tells us that we are distasteful and selfish hedonists if we prefer pleasure to pain. What, if not love and

174

romance, motivates the average couple to establish a permanent relationship, to share their lives with each other? How many wives and husbands can trace the disappearance of love and romance and wanting to be together to the birth of their children? Having time together becomes nearly impossible once you have children. But what is far sadder is that, too often after the children come, a husband and wife may start avoiding time together.

It may seem selfish and irresponsible to wish that love and romance would stay in a marriage. But that indictment can only be made by a society that sees parenthood as an inexorable goal. Because, and there are millions of marriages that prove it, if love and romance are not assured by not having children, their disappearance is maximized by having them.

10
Wrest and
wreckreation

ABOUT THREE WEEKS after we brought Lisa home from the hospital, I was scurrying around getting through the routine of infant care when the phone rang. I recognized the friendly voice of my obstetrician, who said he just called to see how we were getting along. We chatted for a bit, and then he asked, "Have you and Cal gotten out for an evening or you for a day, since the baby was born?" When I told him no on both counts, he said, "I want you to get a sitter, go out with your husband for an evening, get away from the house and the baby, and that's an order!" He went on to say that all new mothers should have time to themselves, away from the house, diapers, baby, and formula, or they'll start feeling depressed and tired. I couldn't imagine leaving my tiny baby with a total stranger and going out and having a good time. But my doctor, seconded by my husband, finally persuaded me that it would be good both for me and the baby to get away from each other. Put in that light, I agreed—if it's good for the *baby,* then I'll go.

I called a local babysitter agency, and stressed that I must have a registered nurse to come in and sit for one evening. Then I grilled the person on the other end of the line about the nurse they were sending.

Satisfied that the agency could provide us with someone qualified to care for our child. I made the arrangements, and the appointed evening for my maiden voyage arrived. On Thursday, March 18, 1965, I left my first child for the first time in the care of another person.

After the nurse arrived, I spent about thirty minutes giving her a rundown of the routine, although there were several sheets of handwritten instructions prepared in advance of the great moment. Finally, quite reluctantly I left the house with my husband, bound for dinner and a movie. We were about three blocks from the house when I finally blurted it out: "She looks like she drinks. A *lot*."

We made it over that hurdle with my husband assuring me that the agency wouldn't send a drunk out to our house to babysit, and he pointed out (rather irrelevantly) that she was wearing a nurse's uniform, so she must be a nurse. We went to the restaurant, had cocktails and dinner and talked about the baby for more than an hour. Before leaving the restaurant, I excused myself to go to the powder room; I went immediately to a pay telephone and called to see if everything was all right (really to see if the nurse's speech might be slurred from raiding our liquor cabinet). At the movies, I felt as if we were three thousand miles away from home. During intermission I excused myself and called home again to see if the nurse were bombed out of her mind.

At the end of the evening I was tremendously relieved to get home and find that the nurse wasn't staggering around, and that my sweet little baby was just fine—Lisa probably didn't even know we were gone. But what an ordeal. An evening out should be relaxing, but how could I relax when I was worrying about my child and feeling like a selfish hedonist who'd neglected a baby to go out and paint the town red?

The next time it was a bit easier. And fairly soon we found some lovely, trustworthy, grandmotherly sitters, so at least we (or I should really say I) didn't worry too much. By the time Adam was born I was more than ready to take off for an occasional evening, or day, but with that readiness to take off a new paradox of motherhood surfaced.

Even though I had the security of knowing that the children were well cared for and that they even liked

179

these nice ladies, I was far from contented. I could be saying to myself that if I didn't get away for a few hours I'd go completely barmy, while having the sinking feeling that I was a terrible mother for wanting to leave my two precious children. That I could admit even to myself that being with them all the time wasn't the ultimate paradise made me feel guilty. To make matters worse, there were those few times that the kids cried at our leaving. Here we'd be on the way out to a movie for the first time in three months, and one or both of our babies would be in tears. It is hard to enjoy yourself when you've just walked out on your crying baby, leaving him unhappy while sloughing off your maternal responsibilities.

A father of two told me that his wife's logic was beyond his grasp. He said she's been complaining that the kids were driving her crazy, so he suggested that she farm them out for a couple of days to a friend who really enjoyed taking them occasionally. She snapped back with, "What? And be away from my babies? Never!" There may be no logic here, but it's true with many of us that while we're *dying* to be away from our kids we feel guilty about wanting to. And curiously, we *do* actually miss them when they aren't hanging around.

Probably, the worst trauma, after that first day or evening out, is the first time a mother is away from her child overnight. One mother confessed that when she went to the hospital to have her second child she felt terrible about leaving her two-year-old. She felt certain that her poor daughter was totally bewildered by her absence and she worried about her constantly.

When a mother leaves her children overnight because she *wants* to, it is, of course, much worse. One young mother, an avid skier, had been counting the days until she and her husband could enjoy a vacation alone in Aspen. After they got back she said they were having a wonderful time, the skiing was great, they were rediscovering each other when she spotted a little girl about the same age as her oldest daughter. That did it. She couldn't wait to get home—suddenly she was missing the kids and feeling unutterably guilty about having left them

180

—even though they were being cared for by a grand-mother whom they adored.

Another mother of two can well afford to go out every night, on weekend trips, and on long vacations with her husband. They don't, of course. It's not that she doesn't like to go out—she loves it. She loves traveling, too. Her lively youngsters frequently drive her nuts, and she admits that she'd love to get away from the routine and the pandemonium. But she can never bring herself to take advantage of all that her affluence allows. She says flatly, "Why, I couldn't *live* with myself if I were always running around and leaving my kids with sitters." The fact is, she rarely goes out and virtually never travels without the kids, and even enjoying her occasional re-spites leaves her with a sense of guilt. This not atypical mother feels guilty about wanting to be away when she's at home and guilty when she is away.

I've never asked a mother how she enjoyed a child-free vacation without getting an answer that was qualified with, "I missed the kids," or "I would have enjoyed it more if I hadn't been worried about Freddie and Julie most of the time."

One friend summed up the feelings of many:

My husband and I have never enjoyed a vacation away from the kids, but about three years ago we both went to New York on business for nine days. I'd never been to New York City, so it was pretty exciting. Until we got to the airport. I wasn't even out of California—not even on the airplane—when it happened; that dull weight sitting on my chest that told me I didn't want to go. My husband managed to get me on the plane, em-barrassed by my tears, and we winged our way to Fun City. It was the most horrible nine days of my life, and I practically kissed the ground when we landed back in San Francisco.

Before we left for New York, my children, then two and six years old, were really getting on my nerves—I was dying to get away. But I called home at least twice a day to make sure they were still alive and to reassure them with my voice on the telephone that I was still alive. And every time I heard their little voices there was a knife in my heart—I missed them so.

I felt incredibly guilty about leaving the kids. What kind of a mother goes off for nine days and leaves her little baby children at home? A bad mother, that's what. But probably the most irrational thought I had during the trip had to do with my being a white-knuckles flyer. I have no faith that a plane can stay up in the air; then there's the danger of mid-air collision, to say nothing of planes being hijacked. In the good old days I just used to worry about dying. But once I became a mother I worried about turning my children into *orphans!* Can you imagine how the poor little things would feel? They're robbed of their parents, and they wouldn't even understand that their Mom and Dad didn't leave them intentionally. I picture them emotionally crippled for life by being permanently rejected at a tender age by their parents. Rest in *peace?* Not possibly.

But only 14 percent of the American public has ever been on an airplane, so we'd do well to get back down to earth to see how most people spend vacations. Even if they can get over the guilt of leaving their kids, most parents feel that children are entitled to a vacation, and since few middle-class couples can afford to take two vacations, it's a pretty safe bet that once the kids arrive, vacations are for the whole family.

This is the way a mother of four describes her annual vacation:

My husband likes to fish, and we can't afford to do much else, so every year we go camping for about two weeks. I wash, iron, fold, and pack just about every summer garment owned by every member of this family. Then I dig out the camping cutlery and dishes, Thermos bottles, and, of course, the chemical toilet. My husband sees to the tent, sleeping bags, and, of course, the fishing gear. We finally load up the station wagon, drive for about five hours, and after three dozen stops along the way, we reach our destination.

The first day or so is actually nice. *Any* change of

182

scenery for me is refreshing. But after about a week of cooking over an open fire, boiling water to do dishes, enjoying the privacy and convenience of our chemical toilet, bathing in the icy water of a nearby stream, and washing clothes on the rocks, I yearn for the dull routine of our suburban house with its indoor plumbing, dishwasher, washing machine, dryer, *hot* water, television set, and telephone.

At least at home when I can't take the confusion, I can escape by turning on the TV or calling a friend. Here there's no escape. The kids flit through the woods and swim in the stream, my husband relaxes with his fishing pole, and I wash diapers on the rocks; the vacation's hardly a treat for me.

We saw some friends recently whom we hadn't seen for a few years and we got to talking about vacationing with the kids. Remembering that they all used to go camping a lot, I said, "But you two really *enjoy* your family vacations don't you?" I based that on the cheery postcards, letters, and snapshots they'd sent from Yellowstone, Vancouver, and wherever they traveled. They said they'd "enjoyed" it so much that they'd quit trying. They'd really done it for the children and now that the kids were getting older and weren't all that interested, they were relieved to be free of the ordeal. What had appeared to be pleasant vacations were, as they said, "endurance contests."

The closest we get to camping is the Annual Company Picnic, where activities include swimming, sack races, baseball, and a good old-fashioned barbecue. Other activities include lost children, bee stings, crying children, fighting children, cut knees, bumped heads, and an occasional domestic quarrel on the way home. The last time we went, Lisa got lost, Adam threw a tantrum, one father got so exasperated with his children that they left early, and three kids got stung by bees. By the end of the day, all the parents looked utterly exhausted, while all the young childless couples were making plans for the evening. The contrast between parents and non-parents is so striking at these functions, I marvel that those who haven't started families yet don't pick up on it. I want to say to them: "Here it is; take a good look. Do you want to look like a raving maniac? Okay, go ahead and keep making plans for your storybook lives, but you have a perfect opportunity today to see what it's like."

Thinking I'm the only uptight mother, I generally look at the others to see if they're enjoying themselves. I derive some kind of comfort from noting that all the other mothers seem to be just as miserable. Everywhere, I see mothers looking for lost children, yelling at kids, taking kids to the bathroom, changing diapers, getting someone something to eat, or just sitting tensely waiting for something else to go wrong.

Knowing that this day is for the children—that my sole function is one of supervising my kids while they're having a good time—keeps me from being frustrated while I'm trying to talk to someone or swim or even eat. I just go along as an attendant, and the greatest reward the day can bring for me is that Lisa and Adam don't get stung by any bees, don't get sick from too much soda pop, don't slug it out with each other, and do have a nice time.

The company picnic is a lot like family get-togethers in the summer. My parents have a swimming pool and they enjoy having the children and grandchildren come over on the weekends—at least I think they enjoy it. Mom always fixes plenty of food, and when we're ready to eat, Dad barbecues hamburgers and hot dogs, and both of them make sure we all eat too much. The kids swim and play ball, trample Grandpa's prize begonias, and put garbage in the swimming pool. When our two were younger there was the ever-present concern that they'd get into the pool while my back was turned and quietly drown while I was laughing at the punch line of a good story. It's difficult to socialize while you're watching children, and besides they want to be in the pool constantly, so that's where you'll find Mommy. As my nephew's wife, the mother of an eighteen-month-old, put it. "You just never relax once you have kids, do you?" And then she ran off to keep her daughter from toppling into the deep end of the pool.

A new mother of a nine-month-old described traveling with a baby: "First there's the question of packing—even for a day—diaper bag, plenty of diapers, bottles, seven changes of clothes, blankets, playpen, a suitcase stuffed with baby toys. Taking the baby *anywhere* for a visit is a very complicated process. Once I get there, I spend most of my time following my crawler around to make sure he doesn't destroy himself, pull over any lamps, or get into mischief; the rest of my time is spent changing diapers, cleaning up spills, and finally packing it all up to return home after an exhausting day of relaxation."

It's hard to believe that one tiny human being needs so much junk—even for a short visit to a friend's house, a picnic, or an outing in the park. Sometimes the advance planning is enough to make you think twice about even going. After Adam was born, whenever we went out, I'd pack a very large suitcase with enough diapers and clothes for two kids, take a sheet for the crib, blankets, toys, bottles, and of course the portable crib. My husband and I would each make a couple of trips to the car to load up for a fun day, pick up our kids and be exhausted before we even got started. Then we'd go off for a day of diapering, feeding, supervising, and cleaning up at someone *else's* house, and if it were a really good day or evening some snatches of conversation would get sandwiched into the routine of child care. If anyone wonders why the station wagon is popular even with small families, there's the answer: You don't get big cars to seat lots of people—you get them because you need a van for all the gear.

One friend who feels housebound put it this way, "By and large, the run-of-the-mill friends don't ask you over all that much after you have kids, because those very people who spend a lot of time questioning you about when you were going to start your family don't invite you over for fear you might bring the kids along—and they're too gracious to tell you to leave them home."

For a lot of people, having friends in is a lot easier than going out. But not that easy. One mother who used to entertain a lot and still likes to have people over said,

185

"Most of the time when we've planned an evening with good friends, I wind up vowing to my husband that I'll never try it again. Once it was a snap to put together a luscious dinner, lay a beautiful table, get the house whipped into shape, and have time to spare; now I feel lucky if I get anything cooked in advance and manage to be dressed on time. I'm no longer fool enough to think the house can look neat and clean even if I spend the day cleaning it, because children live in this house—they do much more in this house, too. During the day I plan and make initial preparations for dinner, straighten up the house, and make a futile attempt at doing something about my appearance. Whether anything gets accomplished seems to depend on the phase of the moon. Sometimes the kids will be completely absorbed in their own activities, there'll be only a few mishaps, and the requests for food and watering will be reasonable. Other times I find my once-efficient self in the middle of disaster minutes before the guests arrive, with cut knees and bumped heads, dinner not started, still in my crummy work clothes, and the house looking like a before picture from *Better Homes and Gardens*."

The mother of a rambunctious and demanding seven-year-old took another route: "We haven't had anyone over for cocktails or dinner since he was three—anyone who isn't really close to us, that is. It simply wasn't worth it."

We haven't given up yet, and we won't, because having friends over is not only something we enjoy, but one of our primary sources of recreation—and the one most parents can best afford. But it's a lot different from before. One friend echoed my thoughts precisely when she said, "I can manage to get things together somehow, but there's still the two hours between greeting the guests and saying the last good night to the children. It may sound petty, but I'd so like to spend an evening entertaining friends that's unpunctuated by having children running in and out with bits of the day they want to share, or requests for glasses of juice they must have or die, or a mad desire to eat up the nuts."

186

Evenings out have proven most revealing. In the middle of one pleasant party, one mother was saying to another, her voice quivering. "What do you do when you come home and find your babysitter doing the laundry at one end of the house, and your ten-year-old drunk at the other? I really shouldn't be here—I feel rotten. I'm so worried about him, and somehow I just feel that if I were a better mother he wouldn't be so difficult to handle. What worries me is that this kid is smart; and he's curious —there's no end to what he might try." They wouldn't have come to the party, she explained, if it hadn't been a very special occasion; they would leave early; she felt guilty for even being here. "Oh, I made sure he's in good hands, of course, but I don't know, this thing is just weighing too heavily on me now."

And somewhere else a mother was telling a nonparent to think about it as she said, "I'm so depressed and worried over our daughter, I can hardly think straight, let alone enjoy myself. I had a meeting with her teacher last week and I can't get it off my mind. I just know that there is something very wrong."

Then this exchange between a husband and wife: "Where are you going?" "To find the telephone." "What for?" "I have to call home to see if everything's okay—the baby looked sort of *funny* this afternoon, and I probably shouldn't have left the house."

There's another kind of relaxation—that of just spending some quiet time alone with your husband. Those moments do exist, they can be caught or snatched. And yet so much of the spontaneity is gone—and not merely the spontaneity of picking up on a moment's notice to go off to the movies. So much of the ease of just being together is lost.

And then, of course, there's the last kind of relaxation. A mother needs some time just to read a book, to sit and recoup the day's energy drain, to be her own person once in a while in her own house. In the best of all possible

187

worlds, at least for me, relaxing and not being obligated even to think about anyone else or about any problems for just a few snatches of time here and there would be the nicest in my own home. Not having to leave the scene physically in order to leave the scene. It would be pleasant if my home were not always merely my place of employment.

Being on call twenty-four hours a day is something you adjust to. As one woman put it, "There are no weekends for mothers." When two adult parents are sitting and reading after the children have gone off to bed, if a child cries or needs something, it's almost always the female adult who heeds the call. Sometimes the other adult doesn't even look up from the newspaper, and most often the child calls for his mother.

The mother of three children, age three, six, and nine, described a typical evening at her house:

> After getting dinner, the dishes, and the kids' baths out of the way, feeling that I'd somehow miraculously survived this particularly chaotic day, I sunk tiredly into the sofa in the living room, and for a moment forgot my exhaustion and tension. I just sat enjoying the record my husband had put on. As I was finally starting to relax and feel human, the mood was shattered by a very loud and, as always, insistent *"Mommy!"* coming from the vicinity of the back hall.
>
> Feeling a perhaps unwarranted amount of self-pity, I got up and trudged off, along the way cursing every expert on motherhood who positively and pompously declares that all mothers should take time out for themselves—that to pursue interests, have time alone with their husbands, and time to relax is not only good for mommies, but for the little ones, too. Along with being annoyed at being disturbed and interrupted yet again, I felt ashamed of myself for having such selfish thoughts.
>
> If this kind of thing happened once a day, I wouldn't have thought anything about it; ten or twelve times— many more times even wouldn't have made me feel as if I were being attacked or punished even when I

hadn't done anything to deserve disciplinary action. But the threshold had been reached somehow, and I'd gone past my normal tolerance level for routine interruptions. And those moments for myself while I was enjoying eight bars of music were well deserved and well earned. Stripping it away just then was like stripping me away *personally*. Pointing out to me that I don't really count, that time for me isn't even *secondary* to the needs, wishes, and whims of my family are these instances: instances where I have every reason to believe that I can relax only to have it demonstrated to me clearly that it isn't so. I resent this and I feel guilty over my resentment.

One mother said that on most days, when a child interrupted her to tend a cut knee or soothe a bumped head, she would respond immediately with concern, yet at other times she was shocked to realize that she felt annoyed. She felt incredibly guilty. "What kind of a mother," she asked, "could feel annoyed when her child is hurt?" She wasn't even doing anything *important* when she reacted this way.

So many women express annoyance at being interrupted, prefacing their statements with some variation of "No sooner do you just sit down, when . . ." or "I'd just sat down to watch the Mike Douglas Show . . ." or "I just got comfortable sitting in the yard . . ."

I wonder if we could be trying so hard to hang on to some part of ourselves that reading a book—just simply reading a book and finishing it—becomes important to us as a kind of proof that we do still have some control over our lives and our destinies. That doing the thing, while important, is not the issue, but retaining the capability to do it is essential.

The mother of small children watches many of her freedoms go as her children grow and create a new array of demands. The big freedoms go all at once, but most parents are prepared to be tied down—even an idiot knows you can't just walk out of the house any time you feel like it. And restrictions on the budget are relatively easy to understand and accept. Yet it comes as something of a surprise that it's difficult to pursue simple hobbies like sewing and painting because doing these things requires your full attention and because some of the tools are dangerous to have within reach of young children.

The loss of privacy starts when your first child starts walking, and the loss grows. Some people dream of going to Hawaii to get away from it all. I just hope that someday I'll have privacy in the bathroom. Being able to simply sit and listen to music without interruption disappears, as does the chance to read a book when you want to— sometimes even finishing a short article becomes difficult. (How many of us have started to read an article, gotten interrupted, and by the time we got back to it found that the magazine had been thrown in the garbage?) Obviously, no job allows a person to do whatever he wants whenever he wants to do it. But few jobs outside of motherhood have as part of the job description that there is no time off—or rather, that there is little time off, but at the full discretion of the employer, and with no advance warning. As one friend put it: "It's not that I can't do what I want—I *can* read a book, I *can* listen to a record. It's just that I can never do it when I want to."

Do we perhaps develop a fear that we will suffer the ultimate loss when we are deprived of a moment's relaxation when we *want* to have it and have worked for it? Do we then lose the last vestiges of self?

11

They are worth their weight in gold

ACCORDING TO A STUDY prepared for the President's Commission on Population Growth and the American Future, it costs the typical American family between $80,000 and $150,000 to rear two children and put them through two years of college. The cost of that first child is estimated at $98,362, if the loss of the mother's earning power is included.[1]

"You can raise a child on a basis quite a bit short of having a silver spoon in his mouth and spend $50,000 at it," says child-development counselor Mrs. Kathy Dunsmuir of Arlington, Virginia. Travel, recreation, and special tutoring can drive the total for one child up to $75,000 or $100,000 with no strain. Parents honestly want to give their children the best, but what exactly "the best" is tends to get obscured.

The baby sell that comes after you've been sold on the idea of having a baby is a fine example of clever merchandising. It closely resembles a tactic admittedly used by philanthropic fund-raisers: "The only way you can get money out of people is to shame them into contributing." And *no* cause can compete with a person's own child.

Parents have the usual amount of human guilt in varying degrees, frequently heightened by feelings of uncertainty and inadequacy about their capability as parents. And so they make excellent targets for this technique. The guilt, reinforced by the sincere desire of most parents to give their children the very best, results in a dream for professional merchandisers.

Leaf through any magazine and count the ads telling you that baby's future will be more secure if you take out a policy with Blank Insurance Company; note those that talk about how Dad was disabled for life, but because he had insurance, his family will be taken care of. Then look for insurance ads that tell new parents how to provide for that necessary college education for their two-week-old offspring. Anything, from cookies to air conditioning units, is sold with the underlying message: "You're a bad parent if you don't buy it. Your children will be less happy if you pass it up."

The real baby-product sell starts taking hold when a woman becomes pregnant. Before the baby arrives, the expectant parents are buying cribs, cradles, bathinets, strollers, baby carriages, diapers, nighties, bottles, and sterilizers. After the baby is born, new parents discover they "need" many more things. While Dad is running to the store to pick up the forgotten cotton swabs or some extra diapers, the homestead is being bombarded. Three days after the birth announcement appears in the newspaper, your mail box is stuffed with free samples of formula, baby food, baby powder, and douche powder; letters and cards from insurance salesmen, baby furniture companies, baby clothing stores, photography studios, and the publishers of sex manuals (I was surprised at that one, too), with the accompanying promise of a free gift for purchasing an item or for agreeing to meet with a company representative. Then there are the phone calls (one day shortly after I arrived home from the hospital with my first child I logged eleven phone calls peddling all of the above, plus some new items like subscriptions to ladies' magazines and books on child care).

One call was from a baby-furniture company representative who told me that she had a free gift for our baby and a film strip to show, at our convenience, on child care and safety. Being very large on anything free and extremely eager to be excellent parents we thought it was terrific.

The appointed evening arrived and at 7:30 we opened the door to a charming woman carrying an audio-visual rig. She set up her gear and started the film on "safety." The first frame showed a stroller with sturdier wire wheels than were on my car. A well-modulated male voice talked to us from the speaker about the stroller's durability, explaining that it wouldn't collapse and break every bone in baby's body. The next frame showed the same thing only it was much taller. The voice explained that the stroller became a cradle. I see. Suddenly a baby carriage appeared on the screen and we were told that with the simple addition of a few components the stroller-cradle became a baby carriage. The announcer described the excellent brakes—no matter what its function at any given time we could be comforted to know that the stroller-cradle-carriage would not roll down a hill. The guarantee covered so long a period of time that I wondered if after eighteen years it might turn into Junior's first car.

But the last frame was the best. Suddenly, the "baby carriage" was stripped of handle and hood, a floor-length, ruffled, synthetic organdy skirt appeared, and *voilà!*—a fancy bassinet. I stole a glance at my husband, and I saw it coming. He really tried, but he laughed so hard he couldn't talk. Then I started. Finally our poor representative started laughing too and, when we all quieted down a bit, she said, "I guess it *is* pretty silly." Then, looking meaningfully around the room at our antiques, art, and book-lined shelves, she took a hard look at both of us and said, "I should have realized—you're not exactly naïve kids." As we laughingly showed her and her equipment to the door, I asked her, as an aside, what that thing cost. She responded reflexively, "Only $499.95, and you can put it on a contract."

What had seemed so amusing that night was enough to enrage me the next evening. My husband came home and reported that two of the men he worked with had bought these things. The men were very young, and they each grossed only about six hundred dollars a month. They could no more afford that baby carriage than we could afford a Rolls Royce. And yet they had each spent five hundred dollars on something they hadn't needed. Because a master of merchandising had been able to convince them that to do otherwise would be to deny their babies the very best and safest equipment. Safe equipment, it should be noted, does not have to cost anywhere near that amount.

Fear of physical harm to one's child is hardly the only fear waiting to be tapped. A friend of mine named Mary, whose circumstances could best be described as impoverished, felt very guilty when her kids were about four and six years old. She kept getting hit by the encyclopedia salesmen. One time, while she was fretting over some dental bills, a saleswoman peddling the *Book of Knowledge* happened upon the threshold, and after my friend said "No, we can't afford it," the woman cast her eyes downward and made gentle, sad noises about how deprived the kids were going to be. Mary wondered for a moment if, in fact, books weren't more important than teeth—only for a fleeting moment—and then she justifiably slammed the door. Mary, of course, never even began to wonder if something for herself or for her husband might be more important.

I remember once explaining to a salesperson (who, incidentally, had fraudulently gained entrance by saying she wanted to discuss the community's educational programs) that we could not afford a four-hundred-dollar set of children's encyclopedias. She was eying our living room, and I found myself stupidly telling her that we really didn't have any extra money, and that our house was once a commune for students, and "it has termites" and "it was such a wreck that we got it for a song."

Keeping up with the Joneses frequently means keeping your baby up with the Jones baby. A wild oneupmanship flowers. Babies don't seem to care particularly if they're dressed in terry cloth from Macy's or organdy from I. Magnin's, but mothers frequently do.

When my children were little, I spent a lot of time with other mothers and, naturally, we all compared notes on child care, giving one another tips and advice on what products were good and what methods worked well and we tried to outdo one another at mothering. We started thinking about the development of our babies' little minds, which led to discussions of books to read, nursery schools, and toys. Toys were discussed very seriously because they are, it is felt, learning tools. A whole new world of peer pressure, competition, and high prices opened up.

There's a line called Creative Playthings, whose catalogue is incredible—it pictures the most prestigious toys right along with some very prestigious prices. Creative Playthings toys are discussed in reverent tones, touted as splendid teaching aids for the very young, and, by implication, for only the very elite. Somehow unreached, I courageously set the catalogue aside and, much to the disdain of our friends, went to a discount store to buy my kids their blocks and other little-kid toys. But the catalogue was nothing to the store that sells these C.P. goodies. The place was exquisitely appointed with deep, shaggy carpets, lots of natural wood, and elegant light fixtures. The saleswomen seemed to convey politely that they would grace you with assistance if they deemed you, the customer, an intellectual and social equal—an impression confirmed by a number of my more candid friends. The message was clear that kids who had these toys would have some sort of educational and social head start over those whose toys came from Sears.

Many people who drive inexpensive compact cars, watch the food budget judiciously, and join babysitting co-ops to save money, spend three or four times as much on a simple set of building blocks or a puzzle labeled as having superior educational merit than they would on an ordinary similar plaything.

I've seen young parents spend money on an extravagant toy while they were worrying about paying the rent. But even those couples who can well afford it shouldn't be coerced into purchasing things children can't possibly appreciate.

Our children have not been deprived of Creative Playthings, and other exciting and sophisticated imports. Chic friends always select these things as birthday and Christmas presents, not wanting us to feel that they'd give our children the low status stuff. But the children, unimpressed by educational merit, superb design, and affirmations of good taste, have, as every child I've ever known, managed to break those toys just as fast as the dime store variety.

A friend of mine reported that the last time she got sucked in by the better-toy gimmick was when she bought her son the most beautiful set of boxes in boxes. They were imported from Germany, made of fine woods, put together in a tong-and-groove fashion, and were beautifully varnished. Overlaid on the lovely finish of each one was a scene depicting a different fairy tale, and there were enough boxes so that all of the classical tales were present and accounted for. The last time she saw even one of the boxes, her child was using it for a watering can while tending a flower he had planted.

It is an aside, but certainly the kids must get the message that something is wrong if they're not keeping up with the Jones kids: "I got a shiny new bike for Christmas, seven wooden soldiers, and a telescope; you only got a *used* bike."

The President's Commission on Population Growth and the American Future tells us what we can expect to spend, on the average, to take care of the necessities for our kids. In *The Baby Trap,* Ellen Peck gives an excellent rundown of how much we can spend if we're less than wholly economically sober.[2] But there is one area of great expense that seems to have been neglected in the literature—the high financial and emotional cost of child-generated destruction.

A child doesn't really get expensive until he's been around for a couple of years—that is, of course, if you resist buying silly furniture, expensive clothing, and "in" educational toys and if you discount the fact that an addition of one or two to the family frequently means an addition in the cost of larger living space and loss of mother's income.

The real increase starts when the kids are about three or four years old, big enough and imaginative enough to make very short work of a very large sofa, dismantle appliances, pull out newly planted trees and shrubs, and devastate their own and their parents' clothing.

There's no way that any material object can possibly mean more to another human being than his own offspring. For us, as for almost all parents, our children occupy the first place in our hearts—they come before anyone else or anything imaginable. But, like most human beings, we feel unhappy when we see our possessions vanishing at a rate that resembles a geometric progression. And, really, our kids are no more destructive than other kids—they're better than most.

Surely I'm only human in feeling resentful that my little boy took an antique cameo ring given to me by my ninety-year-old grandmother. It is (wherever it is) a thing of real beauty, and certainly I was sentimentally attached to it. He did admit to taking it (at least he's honest), but he couldn't remember just what kid it was he traded it to for a toy car. I canvassed the neighborhood in the vain hope of recovering the last of Grandma's treasures, all the while recalling that she gave it to me because she knew I'd cherish it. Maybe a few mothers value a million rings or a million dollars more than their children—I'm not one, but still I do value lovely things, and I can hardly feel *bland* about this loss.

My husband has few hobbies now that we have kids. He doesn't play golf (it's too expensive), we can't afford to go out much, either separately or together, and he doesn't have the time he once had. But he loves photography and music. It's taken us years to buy, piece by piece, the components for his sound system, and I hardly think he's a hedonist for feeling that this is one of his two most cherished material possessions. He buys a few records now and then, I buy him a few, and I always tell friends and relatives who buy him presents that he would like a certain record to add to his collection. Imagine, then, how

198

he must have felt when our young son completely destroyed his turntable, and then one year later destroyed its replacement. Loving Adam is quite separate from the justified distress that made him say, "Jesus Christ, Shirl, can't I have *anything?* Don't I count at all?" (That happened right after his camera was destroyed by the simple quick touch of a child's probing hand.) The point is scarcely that a camera or a turntable or a diamond means more than a child. But we are all human and we all tend to feel frustrated when our possessions are destroyed.

Is it too difficult to understand the frustration of having to spend one hundred dollars to replace a plate glass window the same week the budget has revealed that it's time to tighten up? And that the reason it's time to be careful is that there was a twenty-dollar plumbing bill caused by some little innocent tossing wooden blocks in the toilet, and two weeks before that the toaster toasting marshmallows met an irreparable end and had to be replaced, and just before the toaster said bye-bye, the electric range had to be repaired because someone cooked plastic blocks in plastic pots while Mommy was getting herself showered and dressed.

A friend put it this way: "I love them, but I get absolutely livid—struggling with a diminishing budget and imagining that our entire home will be just a memory soon. When our dishwasher was completely deactivated because our son tossed some plastic toys in while it was running, we'd been saving to buy a new tape recorder—a new one to replace the one that had been destroyed by a child's curiosity. We replaced the dishwasher and did without the tape recorder for a while longer, and the next thing to go was the TV set."

It's important to realize that we're talking about the destruction of the major sources of recreation for many couples. Because of the expense of rearing young children, because the earning capacity has been cut in half with one partner home all day instead of working, they can rarely afford babysitters, movies, and dinners out.

Another mother put it this way, "I *know* Grandma didn't have a stereo or a TV set, but I'm not Grandma.

Maybe we *are* materialistic today and maybe it's wrong. But we don't stop being materialistic just by giving birth. I feel I lose a little of myself every time something of mine is destroyed. I remember when my sewing machine —my friendly mechanical companion for many years, the one material possession that has saved me literally thousands of dollars and given me thousands of hours of pleasure—met its end. The thing *looks* fine, but it's been rendered inoperable by four tiny, curious, exploring hands. The solution is: Buy a new sewing machine. My considered answer is: We can't afford it."

This sort of destruction lasts for only a short time—say about five or six years per kid. However short this period may be, the adults being stripped of their accumulated and worked-for possessions can feel as if their very essence as individuals is being methodically taken from them. They can become quite paranoid about each new disaster, large or small. One woman with enough money to replace every object destroyed by her children put it this way: "You can be determined to remain a self, to have productive interests or interests that just provide simple leisure pleasure, and at each turn you become more apprehensive that something else has disappeared or has been destroyed."

Much more than the dollar count, although that has to be considered, is the feeling that there are forces out to deprive you of any fulfillment or pleasure you seek as a person. You may begin to wonder if the next thing you reach for will simply vanish before your eyes. One asks then, why even try, only to be frustrated.

Items that are neither very expensive nor apparently vital to the perpetuation of self can become incredibly important when wantonly destroyed. A very loving parent can feel resentment over something as trivial as the disappearance of a twenty-nine-cent comb, possibly because it's one more indicator that no longer is the parent important as a person. The source of rage and hurt can be as simple as a thirty-three-cent snapshot—if it just happens to be the only picture you have of a deceased friend or relative.

The other day, it was my last corn pad. I was absolutely furious; I was frustrated; I was annoyed. The last corn pad can mean a great deal to someone about to put on a pair of closed shoes, but nothing to someone guilty of using it in place of Scotch tape to keep a piece of paper attached to the wall.

"We couldn't keep band-aids in the house," said the mother of three grade-schoolers. "When my daughter was seven years old, she put them on imaginary cuts, and she put them on her dolls. I'd discover that we'd run out when I needed one to put on a bleeding knee or elbow."

It's amazing how the disappearance of the Scotch-tape dispenser, the stapler, pens, pencils, or paper clips can cause total exasperation to the point of near rage. It makes you feel quite insecure when even the tiny symbols of your habits keep vanishing. A frustrated adult can waste hours in a determined search for something as trivial as the stapler. One father of four firmly (and, oddly enough, proudly) announced that there would be no TV-watching in his home until the scissors were returned to their proper place. He said he was sick and tired of never being able to lay his hands on something he needed because someone who really didn't *need* the thing had not only taken it, but had failed to bring it back.

It can be a can opener, Scotch tape, the broom, the dust pan, the stapler, pliers, pins, socket wrenches, a comb. It's not so much the loss of the needed object itself that drives you mad, but the fact that nearly every elementary endeavor becomes a monumental task because you can no longer lay your hands on the simple tools you need to carry out simple jobs.

Of course there are solutions. Scissors *can* be attached to chains. Can openers *can* be put on the top shelves of cabinets. Turntables *can* be put behind locked doors. Yet even the most organized households suffer raids by the children. And none of the solutions seems to offer the advantage of living in a way one might wish to live. It is, after all, a bother to trek to the top shelf of the hall closet to get out your makeup each morning. How much more convenient to keep it in the bathroom or on the dresser.

And how do you teach children respect for other people's property when you convey with a series of locks that you don't trust them? And what happens when the phone rings in the middle of locking something up and the forbidden object becomes available and tempting?

When the children were very young and I completely child-proofed our house, my morning routine looked like this: To take my thyroid pill, I stood on a chair so I could reach the top shelf of my closet to get the pill out of a locked case. Then I unlocked the bathroom door, having first unlocked the linen closet to get a towel, remembering to lock it afterwards. Then I took my two-minute shower, hastily dried myself, and threw my clothes on. After that, I got my makeup down from the top shelf of the closet, and proceeded to put on my face. During the entire ritual, of course, I had to return everything to its proper place, put chairs back in order, and make sure everything was once again locked up. A year or so of that is not so bad—maybe. But five years of it doesn't make for relaxed living.

There *are* solutions, but none that seems to allow for civilization and happiness—for the feeling that a home is for the whole family. To solve the problem of property damage (you can't put the sofa on the top shelf of a closet), one couple outfitted their home in furniture the Salvation Army would turn up its nose at; all of it sat on concrete floors that could be hosed down. They both said, almost in unison, "We have a great house. We plan to decorate it tastefully after the kids are grown and gone." True, there's nothing a kid can wreck. Also, true, there's nothing for the parents to enjoy.

Another couple went to the other extreme. Their son is allowed only in his bedroom, the hall bathroom, the family room, and the kitchen of their beautifully furnished home. The boy, so clean and cowed seems less than happy.

Two couples with kids solved this dilemma in the same way; they both have split-level homes. The upper level is adult territory, the lower level is for the kids, or, as one of the mothers put it, "Civilization is up here, the cave is down there."

Sometimes the resentment over the loss of an object is all the more galling when love for the children figured so strongly in owning it. One Christmas season before we had children, my husband and I found an exquisite crèche in a little antique store. The manger was made of wood and straw, and the figures were ceramic and beautifully painted. The crèche came from a small village in Italy, and we were told that the village had since been flooded and that the craftsmen who made the figures had died or disappeared. No more of these would ever be available.

The proprietor of the shop treasured the crèche. He seemed about to refuse to let it go after he told us the story, but he relented when he realized that we appreciated its beauty as much as he did. With a deep sigh, he carefully wrapped each figure, boxed up all the pieces, and wished us a Merry Christmas.

When we got home, we unwrapped everything carefully, set up the figures and manger, and talked about the day when we would have children. As we readied the place of the season and sipped our hot-buttered rums, we talked about the fun and the fullness that would be ours when we were truly a family. We talked about how much our children would enjoy the tradition of putting this together each year.

And after the children were born, putting up the crèche at night and enjoying their reaction in the morning became a part of our happy Christmases. A few nights before last Christmas, we waited until the children were in bed, and then contentedly set about our sentimental task, anticipating the smiles of delight when Adam and Lisa would wake up and discover this annual surprise. We spent wonderful family moments as they asked the questions about each figure the next morning.

Two days later, the children were peacefully sitting and coloring in the room where the crèche was. I was clearing up the breakfast dishes, when suddenly a wrestling match broke out. Before I could get there, the Three Wise Men and two sheep had made it crashingly to the floor.

203

Five ceramic figures do not constitute a tragedy, but as I was picking up the pieces, I remembered our conversation the day we bought this last-of-a-kind Christmas decoration—the conversation about how wonderful it would be to share the crèche with our children.

The feeling of embarrassment when your child destroys a friend's possession perhaps can be dismissed as vanity. The destruction of material goods, however vital to the pleasure of the individual parent or the total family, perhaps can be disregarded as crass materialism. The feeling that one's self is being stripped away with each new depredation or disappearance perhaps can be tossed off with an accusation of a neurotic attachment to objects. It could be said, quite validly, that a destructive dog could do as much harm. Yet all of the above feelings exist and are caused not by dogs, but by children. And perhaps what hurts the most is the feeling of frustration and failure that comes to parents as they wonder if their children can possible be growing up with a regard for other people's property, as they watch their own disappear.

12

Doctor, lawyer Indian chief ... or mother

FROM THE TIME Lisa was born, my husband and I talked about my going back to work. I liked working, we both felt my training and experience should not be wasted, and we could always use more money.

I went back to work full-time at a job I found consistently interesting and challenging when Adam and Lisa were in nursery school a couple of days each week. My daily routine consisted of getting up at 6 A.M., making breakfast, making the beds, doing the dishes, getting myself dressed, leaving a list of instructions for the sitter, talking to the sitter, and finally leaving for the office. When I got home at about 6 P.M. (if I ran errands during my lunch hour), I would spend a few minutes with my sitter—a warm, helpful woman—then with each child. Then I would change my clothes, start dinner, and, because Cal didn't get home before seven, feed the children and get them ready for their baths—a ritual I did not delegate to our sitter because I felt I did little enough mothering.

When my husband arrived I would set the table, have a cocktail on the run, continue bathing the children while making a pass at conversation, get them dried, check their teeth and ears, put on their pajamas, and finally coax them into bed.

We would eat dinner, and afterward I would do the dishes, and Cal would work on whatever projects he had brought home. Then I'd do some laundry, washing and drying and folding as much as possible, check my clothes for the next day, do something to my hair, and finally fall into bed.

My husband is a dear and considerate man, but he had become used to things the way they had been. I could hardly expect him to develop expertise at laundry instantly, and willingly set aside his own work.

Most weekends Cal did the marketing and I cleaned the house and ironed. What left-over time we had was devoted to the loose ends of our jobs and catching up with the children. I assumed that taking the kids to the doctor and the dentist was my responsibility—part of my routine, just as it is with nearly every other working mom I've ever talked to.

When the children entered kindergarten, I learned that there were many functions at the school mothers were expected to attend. The working mother is never exempt as her spouse is. If the kids needed me, I felt it was top priority. Putting together Halloween costumes for them took precedence over doing work brought home. If the babysitter or the school nurse called me at the office a knife went through my heart—part of me was always with the children, however engrossed I was. When I traveled occasionally, it was agony. (Interestingly enough, when my husband travels on business, he doesn't feel that way at all.)

I was called out of meetings so important I left "absolutely do not disturb" instructions—always qualified with "unless it is related to my family." (My husband has never been called away from work in the seven years we have had children.) I once rescheduled a press conference because I had to see the kids off for the first day of school, and I constantly shuffled all my appointments around so that my work would not interfere excessively with my role as a mother.

Once when my daughter was having trouble in school, I could not keep my mind on my work, although there was nothing I could do. A man is conditioned to concentrate on his work and usually can set a personal worry aside to do so; a woman is conditioned to be concerned primarily about her children. It is very hard for a mother to discipline herself not to worry.

All this is part of a mother's career life. It is difficult trying to compete as a woman in a man's world. A woman is expected to be less committed to the job, or less competent than a man. If she is a mother, not only does more doubt about her ability surface, but there is a measure of reality that can't be discounted.

As my children got older, worry about them increased as their activities broadened. When they went to school I started worrying about their intellectual development, their relationship with their peers, the little problems they brought home—so little to adults, but so big to children. While they were happy enough staying with the baby-sitter, they seemed bothered that I left home every day and therefore it bothered me. They wondered why I wanted to leave them; I explained that it wasn't that way —I didn't want to leave them particularly. I just had to and wanted to go to work. They accepted that with their father, but with their mother, they found it troublesome. If the morning before we all left was especially trying, it stayed with me a good part of the day. If one of the kids really felt bad or got on the school bus in tears, that was the picture I carried in my heart when I went to the office.

It bothered the children that I wasn't there when they got home from school, and it bothered me, too. I used to wonder if they felt they weren't important to me, and worried how that might affect them.

Before I had kids, I did what most men do—when I went to work, I worked—I didn't have incredible responsibilities, and I didn't have any guilt feelings about working. I didn't have that little maternal undercurrent going on all the time, occasionally highlighted by crisis and illness.

When I resigned from my job, some of the directors made a lot of noise about getting another woman to replace me so they could preserve their progressive image. I think it's telling that my successor is a bachelor.

The moment a mother decides to venture out into the

working world she must cope not only with the problems of any working woman—the attitudes we're all quite familiar with by now—but with the guilt of leaving her children. She will almost always feel guilty for *wanting* to leave.

Any mother who is committed to a career must be prepared for criticism that does little to relieve her guilt. She must *justify* her decision to become part of the labor force —not an easy task. However, if she becomes involved in a charitable or public service organization, receiving no salary, then a woman is generally considered a credit to her husband, the neighborhood, and the community.

The woman who works because she must is generally excused by her acquaintances and by her children's teachers. I say "generally" because there is a sort of class judgment that underlies the sympathy for such working mothers—how can you criticize such a person for being so responsible, but then, how can you really relate to her as an equal? Many women comment that elementary teachers categorically disapprove of working mothers—a bit strange, since many elementary school teachers are working mothers themselves. Perhaps it helps the pot to call the kettle black.

Also semi-acceptable is the woman who goes to work part-time or who dabbles at working. While not enthusiastically accepted by society, a woman may be able to get away with working some of the time at a not-terribly-onerous job, so long as she makes sure that her commitment to her job does not begin to approach her commitment to her home. Two disadvantages to working part-time have been mentioned by many mothers. First, it is very difficult to find a part-time job that provides any kind of career advancement. Most women found them time-killers and, while many women have found the stimulation of simply getting away from the house beneficial, no woman who had any desire to succeed in her field felt that her part-time work was more than a stopgap. Second, many women found that many of the disadvantages of working full-time—pressures of two jobs, division of commitment, grueling schedules—held true for part-time work. Part-time work, said one woman, "is merely full-time work for part-time pay."

Most women who worked not from financial need, but because they wanted to gave as their reason the desire to do something other than mothering. Salaries for most women are so low that, when the costs of working are deducted, many find that working is costing them money. If her husband is the least bit ambivalent about having his wife work, a good deal of friction can result. Many women said that they worked not because the job itself was so wonderful, but because for all the problems of working, at least it was better than the job they had at home.

But for the woman who works out of choice, who is committed to her work and works full-time and works hard, or for the woman who has not taken time off for a few years while her children are small, the disapproval is far more blatant. Those of us in this category have all experienced the implication from our relatives that we are neglecting our children, and from our neighbors that we are selfish for seeking careers outside of the home, and we have all gotten the old jazz from our kids' teachers—"if you could just give up your career temporarily so that you could spend more time with Freddie, it would help so much—after all, he really needs you now . . ." The unspoken suggestion is that once you don't need the money, you might at least forego your career plans until Freddie goes to college. "Need" here, you must understand, is defined as, say, the difference between starving and not starving—not needing extra money so that the family can have the added freedom and comforts that come with a few extra dollars.

Having overcome her own ambivalence, peer bias, and unwritten discriminatory hiring practices, the working mother must arrange for the care of her children. Finding someone responsible, someone with whom she feels confident about leaving the children, someone the children like is no easy task. School can be counted on for only part of the time—the problem of after-school and vacation time is one working mothers must deal with.

210

And even after satisfactory help is found, the mother cannot rest as easy as her husband, who knows that his children will be taken care of by his wife or by someone hired by his wife. If a mother's help is away, must leave early, or has to be replaced, it is her responsibility to take care of the children or to find someone else. Unlike hiring a new maid or a new secretary, hiring a new sitter for your children takes on epic proportions. She must be so good for the children that you can feel they are not suffering unduly from your absence.

Once Mom lands a job, it doesn't take long to know that she's just made it through the easy part. Let's look at the affluent mother of four. Marcia didn't need the job she sought, but was qualified for it and had her own reasons for leaving Paradise as sold by Madison Avenue.

By the time my youngest was five years old, I was just about going insane. To justify my need to get out of the house, I first went the volunteer route. I hired sitters and did work for several public service organizations and I loved it. One of the organizations needed a public relations specialist and somehow, with my knack for PR and my background in journalism, I seemed to qualify, so I was offered a staff position. I finally decided that once the kids were in school full-time, I'd hire a housekeeper and take the job if they still wanted me. I should mention that my salary passes through my hands and pays for the housekeeper, baby-sitters, expenses, and income taxes.

I started working full-time about a year ago, and it is great. I have many reasons to count my blessings. My husband always has felt that raising the kids is both parents' responsibility, and he does more than just talk a good line. We take turns preparing meals, cleaning up afterward, doing scout things with our son, and going over to the school for all of the meetings. Even before I worked, we had that arrangement. I have a competent housekeeper—and the kids adore her. I don't have to pick up even a dish during the day, but instead I can sit at my desk dreaming up great projects, or I can meet interesting people, or go out to lunch with colleagues. On top of this, my husband and I go on one good vacation every year by ourselves, and we take the kids on a really good trip.

Anyway, what have I got to complain about? Nothing—right? And yet I'm depressed, nervous, and I feel that life is becoming a confused mass of conflicts passing before me. Despite the fact that I have so much to be grateful for, the guilt I feel is intense. Am I being a good mother to the kids? Will my absence from home affect them adversely? And my normal amount of guilt is worsened by having so many advantages. I thrive on my job during the day, love my husband, and only a fool could not love those four lovely kids. But even with help I'm exhausted. Sometimes I think that if I gave up the job I wouldn't be so tired. But then I remember back to the days when I didn't have the job, and I was even more tired and I was a nervous wreck. I think what's eating at me is the fact that I know in my heart I'm not really equipped for motherhood, but the kids are a fact, or rather, four facts, of life, and there's virtually nothing I can do to make myself the sort of person equipped to really handle this responsibility—working or not. I do know that it's much more difficult to work when you have kids, but even with the added strain, I know that it would be far worse not to work.

I can easily resign from my job. I can't resign from hated PTA meetings, Bluebirds for my daughters, scouts for my sons, helping with homework, and the noise they generate with each other night after night. I come home from the office feeling nicely tired after a good day's work and to a full report from the housekeeper. "Mrs. Lewis," she says, "the toilet is running over, Jenny has a fever, the school called because Denny's library books are due back, and also a problem has developed with Debbie. Mrs. Harris, that's Jill's mother, called to remind you that you promised to bake cookies for the Bluebird meeting." While I'm listening to the report, I hear the sounds of my darlings, whom I've actually missed during the day, and soon I hear anything from a "he touched me" battle to "I want to watch 'The Flintstones.' " Suddenly I wish I

212

were back at the office. All the while I'm trying to squeak through the door, set my purse down, and get dinner started, and I get an "ugh, we had that last night" as I get started. I'm probably more sensitive to my kids' complaints because I only get part of them. And I feel guilty that I don't like it.

I remember back to the serenity of my office (which is a pressure cooker) when I hear, "But you prom*mmmised* I could get a new catcher's mitt, you've just gotta take me shopping . . . Raymond took my baseball cards. . . . Denny hit me with the dictionary. I only hit him because he took my baseball cards—give 'em back, give 'em back, Ma, please make him give 'em back." As I sink slowly, I marvel that, when their father gets home, he doesn't take one look and listen for a minute and go back outside the door, get into his car, and leave—never to return again. I'm a mother escaped, but it falls somewhere short of heaven.

Another mother who is making excellent use of her very good education with a magnificent job, has described a routine nearly identical to our previous mother's, and she adds this:

After dinner, we each take two kids on for the homework, and then long after I've noted that it's past *my* bedtime just because I'm wrung out, we prod them into taking their baths, brushing their teeth, going to bed, and somehow get them to stop whispering after the lights are out.

I'm fortunate. Several nights a week, our housekeeper stays on long enough to get dinner and this should really make a difference, but it *doesn't*. If your kids are going to nag you it doesn't matter much if you're sitting down enjoying a drink and waiting for someone else to fix the meal or if you're fixing it yourself. Perhaps "nag" isn't fair—they *do* have questions, and they *do* have things they want to tell you. That I'm not all that interested in what they have to say makes me feel guilty as hell.

Oh, hell, they have rights and needs, and every night I go to bed with one thought when we've gotten through it all—I'm a rotten, miserable mother. I love those kids, they're each unique and wonderful and part of *us,* part of two people who really care about each other. But somehow loving them doesn't alter my basic capabilities when it comes to motherhood. I can't understand how I could be so proficient at my office job on the one hand and so lousy at mothering on the other.

Sonia has only two children. Her mother lives with the family and takes care of all the housekeeping chores. Sonia went back to work after her children were in nursery school. Every day her mother called her at the office to give her a blow-by-blow report on the toilet, the furnace, the cat in the tree, the school problems, and the skinned knees. Finally, Sonia decided it was too much. The combination of the grueling routine (even with just two kids), her mother calling her at the office, her constant worry about the kids and the guilt she felt about wanting to be away from them, got to her, and she decided to quit her job and stay home. Six months later, she was back at work. One year later she was home again. The last time I saw her, her husband had made it really big with an invention and they were, practically speaking, rich. She was talking about getting her old job back, however, but really couldn't justify it this time.

Another mother who has found achieving success at two careers difficult traces her work history.

I was married when I was twenty, straight out of college, and I went to work in advertising. I loved working and I was good at it, rising quite quickly to a solid middle-management position within three years. Then I got pregnant—sort of accidentally on purpose—and, like all nice little middle-class girls who got married, got a nice little job in communications, and got pregnant, I quit. I worked until about a month before the baby was due and I had an absolutely marvelous pregnancy. About two weeks after my baby was born, when we let the baby nurse go, I realized that motherhood was not precisely my cup of tea. But I'd been brainwashed thoroughly and even though I hated taking care of

214

the baby and staying home, I didn't even think about going back to work. After about a year I couldn't stand it any more and I started taking on free-lance assignments. Over a six-year period I had two part-time jobs, one two days a week, one three days a week, lots of free-lance assignments, and another baby. Of course, nothing I did during this period did very much to push me up the ladder in the advertising business, but at least I kept up my contacts and had something to do. Even though I was spending as much time with my kids as non-working mothers, I felt guilty about it, maybe because I knew I hated motherhood and couldn't wait until I could get myself to the point where I could go back to work full-time. I'm extremely motivated, and I got to the point where I couldn't stand it as I saw the years creeping by with me just treading water, amusing myself with playing at work. I wanted to move, I wanted to get ahead, but I was too petrified by the unwritten rule that said mothers stay home when the kids are small. I felt so damned guilty about not liking being a mother that I couldn't compound it by leaving them. And of course I couldn't get anywhere as long as I couldn't bring myself to go back to work full-time. In a lot of ways it was an ideal arrangement. My husband had a fairly decent wife and mother with an outside interest—a nice little adornment for a wife in our group. My children had a mother who could just about stand it because at least she had a little something to keep her going. And I had enough rationalizations to keep me moderately happy.

When my younger child started nursery school half a day, I decided I would go back to work full-time. I had several job offers but every single person who interviewed me and just about all my friends in the business couldn't understand why I wanted to go back to work. Several people suspected my motivation and everyone voiced doubts about whether I really meant it. I have a housekeeper who, while she doesn't do a thing for the house and drives me crazy because she's a mother too, and calls up periodically in the morning to say she can't make it, loves the kids and is loved by them. So I manage to keep my guilt over not wanting to be

215

a mother and preferring to work down to just a medium-high level. I worry constantly that I'm neglecting them, that they're growing up deprived because their mother would just as soon not be with them, and I try to make up for it by being especially wonderful after work and on weekends. Not that I always am, of course. When I look at myself objectively I don't think I'm a worse mother than most. I love them and I'm proud of them and there are times that I enjoy them—more and more as they get older. But half the time when I get home from work the last thing I want to do is turn myself on for my kids. So the old saw about "it's not the quantity of the time, it's the quality" falls flat. Because a lot of the time not only isn't there quantity, there isn't quality either.

My job is an exceptional one for a woman and I love it. I feel as though I'm moving for the first time in years. My work is extraordinarily demanding. To do a halfway decent job I have to work in the evenings and on weekends. I could have taken a less demanding job, but it would have meant forgetting about succeeding.

Wendy, who at thirty-five heads a thriving public-relations firm, had much the same feelings about her children. She had some interesting things to say about her marriage:

What has happened is that I'm used up when it comes time for my husband. He can't quite understand why I have to work so hard—he liked it a lot better when I had a pleasant little part-time job. I think of his demands as excessive, but in my more rational moments I'm not sure that they are. He does, I would think, have a right to a wife. What he has instead is a body that goes through the motions because that's about all she has the energy for. I've thought quite giddily at times that we've completely reversed roles. I'm the tired businessman who's all tied up in his work and has no time for his wife. I have, thank God, an enormous amount of energy, but I feel pulled in a hundred and two different directions. People are always asking me how I do it. On a wing and a prayer and a Librium.

216

Then there is Peggy, a teacher. She loves her work and considers it her salvation. Like Sonia and many others, she has no financial need to work. She has the patience to teach high school students and she loves her kids—her kids being her students. She super-loves her own three kids, but she is quick to say that she realized some time ago that she was not cut out for a career in motherhood, that as difficult as it is being both a teacher and a mother, her life would be empty without her job.

When she gets home in the evening, she must deal with her children's problems at three different age levels; she must worry about the termites, the plumbing, and writing the checks to pay the family's bills. Unlike the childless woman, Peggy, like Sonia, Marcia, and all the other working mothers, no matter what their degree of affluence, goes home to still another full-time job. Peggy is a gifted teacher who feels that she does not have what it takes to be a successful mother. She, like all of the others, will continue to try and continue to feel like a guilty failure.

Phyllis is the wife of a successful dentist. She is also a school teacher and the mother of one child. She says flatly, "One is enough. If I'd had more than that I'd never have been able to teach, and it's only now that she's in college that I'm really able to pursue my career and not be completely worn out by the time I get to bed. I wasn't about to give up teaching. It wouldn't have helped. If I'd stayed home all day, which I did for a time, I'd feel just as frustrated and guilty as I did working. And just as tired."

Some women opt for working at home as writers or painters. "If the creative woman has children," said Marya Mannes, in an article in *Look*, "she must pay for this indulgence with a long burden of guilt, or her life will be split three ways between them and her husband and her work. . . . No woman with any heart can compose a paragraph when her child is in trouble. A man at his desk in a room with a closed door is a man at work. A woman at a desk in a room is available."

One very wise woman said this to me: "I love children

217

and I have many. They are my patients. I had to choose between being a mother and being a doctor. I know I couldn't do justice to both professions at the same time."

Few women, however, have the combination of full-time help and a fulfilling job. Nor do they have the freedom to work or not as they choose. More typical are women like Emma.

Emma is twenty-six years old and has four little stair-step children. She works because she needs the money and she works like the devil to make sure she keeps her job. Every morning, Emma gets up at 5:30 to prepare breakfast for the family, dress the children, comb their hair, get herself dressed with some measure of neatness, put the kids in the car, and take them to the babysitter. She arrives at the office in the nick of time at 9 o'clock sharp. Lunch hour is for running family errands while dashing about with a sandwich. Work ends (such it does) at five, and then her evening begins. She picks up the children, returns home, tosses a load of laundry in the washing machine, prepares dinner, eats, washes the dishes, bathes the children, does some more laundry, does her hair (beauty shops are not in the budget), folds clothes and goes to bed. One or two nights each week are reserved for ironing and housecleaning. She looks forward to her ironing night, because she watches television while she irons and can justify the recreation.

Another woman I used to know, when I worked before I had chiildren, had a job both to supplement the family income and because she loved working. Amy, the mother of three great kids, had a routine similar to Emma's but her job was a bit more demanding. Very often she found herself working six days a week. She was very well organized and not a lot seemed to bother her, although she occasionally commented that she never had time to read or enjoy things other than her job and family. That she really did like her work made up for a lot, but even so, she did get weary, and she was constantly torn between quitting the job, thus lowering the family's standard of living and giving up her one real personal pleasure, and just staying put. The dilemma was settled when the dentist informed her that one child right after the other would need extensive orthodonture.

Amy always kept her sense of humor, although her routine was grueling. She never went to bed before midnight and never slept later than 5:30 during the week. She frequently received phone calls at the office telling her that someone was ill or some minor disaster was taking place at home, and one day I dropped by her office and found her close to tears. She'd been talking to the teacher of one of her children, and there had been a small crisis at school. She couldn't leave the office with any ease (an important meeting was scheduled but she felt that she really should go over. In the end she did just what most mothers do (and few fathers are ever called upon to do): She went to the school. On another occasion she looked unusually tired. I carefully asked if everything were okay, and she told me that her youngest child had been sick all weekend, and the night before she had bundled her up and rushed her to the doctor's office. "She's fine now, but the weekend was pretty scary and tiring."

One morning Amy arrived at the office looking harried and she described a scene I didn't believe until years later, when something like it happened to me. At breakfast, Jimmy had gagged on a piece of toast, triggering one of the other kids, who started gagging; the next kid actually vomited, Dad pushed his dish away and ran for the bathroom and, as she described it, "Here I stood, looking at my pathetic egg, and everyone around me seemed to be in some state of pre-, post-, or otherwise nausea." I roared with laughter as she told it, and then I noted that marvelous Amy wasn't even smiling.

Amy nearly always was able to laugh at her chaotic and exhausting life, but she did want something more; she always wanted to be just a bit more than somebody's something—somebody's mother, wife, or secretary—and she had the talent to bring it off. And yet she said to me often. "I'd even scrub floors at night to pay for orthodonture, education, or anything else my three kids might need."

Many mothers find taking their tearful, pre-school kids to the babysitter each morning painful. Elsa said to me, "He really loves it at Auntie's because he has lots of little kids to play with. But you'd never know it, and it's not very comforting to have my son reproach me tearfully five days each week." As soon as she can afford to, she plans to leave her job.

One working mother who didn't realize the importance of good attendance got herself fired. Pat had two kids in school. She had to go to parent-teacher conferences four times a year, take the kids to the dentist and the doctor, and she felt obligated to go over to the school whenever she was asked. Each child averaged one week of illness and Pat herself suffered from the cold and flu season and from an occasional bout with menstrual cramps. She had to see the dentist and the doctor, and occasionally she took time off for business matters related to running a home. Her absences averaged one day a week, and she was fired. It is to her credit that she never neglected any of her responsibilities as a homemaker and a mother. But in the end it cost her a job.

While the average working mother has to stay home when a child is sick, she seldom can afford the luxury of nursing herself for fear that high absenteeism may lead to dismissal. It is frustrating to try to be all things to all people—children, husband, employer—and wind up being penalized in the end for a valiant effort.

Members of the liberal community and women's liberation in particular view day-care centers and egalitarian marriages as dual solutions to many of the problems of the working mother. Even if a woman is fortunate enough to be married to a man who will divide the drudgery absolutely equally (and such an arrangement is rare), the ultimate division will find her with more than half the share of real and psychological responsibility for the children.

In an article on day-care in *The New York Times Magazine*, William Shannon cites several disparaging studies of day-care that find probable psychological damage to the children. Most telling is his finding that in the Soviet Union, where day-care has been widespread for many years, senior officials who run the centers do not make use of them for their own children, preferring to use their high incomes to employ someone to care for their children at home.[1] While no conclusive study exists, there is enough doubt in many mothers' minds that their children will be happy and secure in a day-care center. One short-term effect was mentioned by Mark, the father of a three-year-old daughter.

His wife is presently finishing her education, carrying a full course load that keeps her away from home all day. He works, so they have placed their little girl in a day-care center for the academic year. Discussing this one day he said. "By the time we take Amy to the center, go our separate ways, and pick her up around 5:30, that poor little kid will have spent about ten hours at the center, and there'll only be time to give her dinner and a bath and put her to bed. Parents considering this for the long haul should really think of what it might mean to a small child."

Do you remember what it was like when you were a little kid—how long an hour seemed? If an hour to a child is such a long time, what in the world might ten hours away from home without a parent seem to a three-year-old?

And Dr. Spock, who once proposed that mothers be paid to stay home and take care of their children, says:

The important thing for a mother to realize is that the younger the child, the more necessary it is for him to have a steady, loving person taking care of him. In most cases, the mother is the best one to give him this feeling of "belonging" safely and surely. She doesn't quit on the job, she doesn't turn against him, she isn't indifferent to him, she takes care of him in the same familiar house. If a mother realizes clearly how vital this kind of care is to a small child, it may make it easier for her to decide that the extra money she might earn, or the satisfaction she might receive from an outside job, is not so important after all. . . . A day nursery or a "baby farm" is no good for an infant. There's nowhere near enough attention or affection to go around. In many cases, what care there is is matter-of-fact or mechanical rather than warmhearted. Besides, there's too much risk of epidemics or colds.[2]

That day-care centers are needed *now* for many oppressed mothers who must work and for many other women who feel that the resumption of their careers is necessary to their well-being is not being debated. But we should not accept either egalitarian marriage, total liberation of women, or the establishment of public-supported day-care centers as the ultimate answer to the question of whether a woman should be a doctor, lawyer, secretary, or mother.

Any woman considering motherhood who would opt for placing a child in a day-care center for ten hours each day should consider more carefully her motives in wanting to have a child. I agree with Dr. Spock that public-supported day-care centers are no substitute for the tender care of a loving and affectionate parent during the crucial months and years when a child is still small. The simple act of changing a diaper for a baby or helping a five-year-old put his shirt on can carry a caress when performed by a loving mother. A parent quite absently weaves acts of affection into simple routine tasks.

Dr. Spock's statement and my seconding of it bring tears of rage to the feminist: It is just this philosophy that has kept women in the home for so many years. And yet, Spock is merely giving voice to the feeling that so many women have, or discover to their discomfort that they have, after they give birth. The mother who feels less than affectionate toward her child may well feel that she would do better to leave the child in the care of someone else. Yet it is a rare mother who can go through the motions, if resentfully, without feeling that she is the best at loving her child. You cannot, after all, hire love. Many women find that the pull of societal conditioning affects them more strongly than they would have expected.

Doing all that they feel they should for their children and doing all that they must to further themselves professionally is an almost mutually exclusive situation.

To the woman who would intentionally pursue two careers, with the full knowledge of what is involved, I have to ask, why in the world do you want children? Because it's the thing to do? Because it *looks* like fun? Because you feel that you'd somehow lead a fuller life? You must think about what it's really like to work all day, leave your children in the care of a probably sterile day-care center, rush over to the center, pick up the little one, race home (if you are lucky) to an egalitarian marriage, spend about two hours with a small bewildered child who needs much more, put him to bed, then go to bed yourself exhausted, only to get up next day and repeat it all. Does that sound like an ideal family life situation?? Or does the scene look more like something out of 1984?

Any childless woman considering combining motherhood and a career should stop and determine which might mean more right now, before the biological facts are in. If you have a career you could test your willingness by interrupting your work for one year. During this period, you could read all of the books that have been published on child care, child-rearing, and troubled children. Actually, the quickest test is to pick up a copy of Dr. Spock's *Baby and Child Care*. Read the book and bear in mind that Dr. Spock speaks of *average* situations and *normal* children.

I do not have a blueprint for an ideal mother. But if I were drafting a job description, I'd start out by saying that her motives for wanting children should not be a result of social pressure or any coercion. I would suggest, too, that anyone "born" to motherhood would not necessarily have to fulfill herself by having a biological child. The ideal mother would be a loving, friendly woman who is patient, likes working with children, likes caring for others, enjoys being around children, and is willing to place the interests of her children above any of her own without feeling that she is making sacrifices.

One of the most successful mothers I have met has no outside interests except for reading and outdoor activities that can be enjoyed with her children. She is by no means a dull person. She knows what is going on in the world, and feels that she must keep abreast of current events, local and international, to be a useful citizen and a well-informed mother. While she is not possessive of her children, her entire day revolves around the family. She is a room mother, a member of the PTA, drives in a car pool, gives three days each week to the cooperative nursery school her youngest child attends, "observes" (parents in our district are invited to come to class frequently and watch their children's performance) at the elementary school her six-year-old attends, helps out with school activities, outings, and field trips. She spends time teaching her children many things like nature studies and swimming. The family camps, hikes, and travels together by car. She is a decent housekeeper, but she's quick to admit that she cleans house and makes beds only in her spare time. To her a shiny floor cannot compete with spending an enriching hour with her kids. She is in excellent health, her children were planned, she has a college degree, and she is not remotely interested in pursuing a career, because she already has one that suits her. She said that she had just two kids (both boys) because she likes children and finds caring for them completely fulfilling. No, they will not try for a girl because she doesn't buy the sex-distribution requirement of the model family. She plainly says a child is a child, and that she never preferred one sex over the other. She and her husband stopped at two because they felt they could adequately handle two; they were not sure they could do a good job if they had to spread their financial, physical, and emotional resources any further than that.

This woman is not nervous, does not appear to be frustrated, laughs easily, and I've never heard her criticize another mother. She *has* said, however, "Motherhood is a tough full-time job and many people aren't cut out for it." That she generally likes children became evident immediately; she's the only mother I've known, not a close friend or relative, who has offered to take my children for full days at a time because, "You have such nice little kids and my kids like them so much." When I balked, the second time she offered, saying it was too much and I should reciprocate, she said "Nonsense—I love being with children."

Perhaps, then, this unusual mother would serve as the model for any guidelines I might propose. At least it's a start. There is no shame in not being maternal material, and, oddly enough, knowing this mother has reinforced my belief that this is true, because she does genuinely enjoy her work. She would not, she admits, if a part of her were yearning to practice law or work in an office.

Perhaps one day we will see total human liberation when men can be "mothers," if they like, without having their manhood challenged, and women who prefer other roles will be able to pursue them without having their worth and womanhood defined only by their aptitude for motherhood. But first, we must free both sexes from being pressured and deluded into parenthood.

For now, motherhood is a career generally reserved for women—it is grueling, painful, formidable, and must be the top-priority job. It cannot take a back seat to any other career. There is nothing that can compete with the importance of another life.

Think about it.

🍓 afterword

THE DECISION TO WRITE *Mother's Day Is Over* came several months after I painfully acknowledged to myself that I didn't like being a mother.

I had brooded over what seemed to be a real contradiction: How was it possible for me to genuinely love my children and yet not like—often to the point of resentment—nearly everything associated with the role of motherhood? It bothered me that I didn't *embrace* being needed by these two young children who needed me so much, that I resented the fact that their demands were so unstructured and their needs so open-ended that I had to organize my activities entirely around theirs. Even a husband pretty much allows his wife to read when she wants to read, to go to the bathroom without holding a running conversation through the door, and generally to remain asleep when she is asleep unless there is a good reason to wake her.

The very act of telling a friend how I felt about motherhood launched the book for me. We had gone to lunch together to discuss some social issue of mutual interest, but we never got around to the agenda. A mother of four, she responded to my honesty by matching it and going even further. After admitting that if she had known how painful motherhood is she would never have had children, she said, "Sometimes I think most mothers feel the way I do, and other times I feel very much alone. Certainly I have never admitted to *anyone* how I feel because I was certain that most people would think I was a heartless and unfeeling woman—an unnatural woman." It was then that I decided to talk with other mothers. Honesty begot honesty, and I truly believe the mothers I talked with derived comfort from learning that many women shared their unhappy plight of feeling guilty for not adoring motherhood.

Since most of the interviewing or just plain talking took place in my home over lunch or coffee, my children started picking up a few ideas. They started questioning what I was doing and how I felt about them. This alarmed me at first, and I nearly abandoned the book for fear that it would cause them to think badly of themselves, not to mention their mother.

But one of the genuine joys of parenthood is that, if we listen carefully, we can actually learn from our children. By explaining to them that they were really a handful and that sometimes I felt sad that I wasn't a better mother, I learned that during my "quiet" years they knew that something was wrong. And unless my intuition was way off, both of them seemed genuinely relieved that it was just that simple. I gathered this not only from Adam and Lisa but from one sixteen-year-old girl who told me, "My mother has never said a word about resenting me and my brother—she's nice to us and tries to be a good mother—but I've always known we were resented." Another teenager told me, "If my mother didn't resent me why does she always make me feel so guilty—like I was doing something wrong even when I wasn't?"

Although I was still a little uneasy about what effect my catharsis might have on the people I love best, one thought kept recurring: the value of honesty—it gets everything out in the open where it can be dealt with. And in being honest, perhaps fuller relationships can develop between all members of my or any family. My relationship with my husband, for example, has improved markedly because we have come to understand each other's fears and doubts about the kind of parents we are. And I am convinced that my relationship with our children has improved tremendously because they no longer

229

worry that something dark and sinister is going on within their mother when she is less than totally jolly; they know it's the *job* of mothering I dislike—not them. I also think I have developed the facility of thinking things through more maturely and achieving better perspective while guiding and disciplining my youngsters.

While preparing this book, I found only six (out of two hundred or so) of the women I spoke with were what I would call truly outstanding parents, fulfilled by their roles and possessing a talent for nurturing and guiding their children in something approaching an inspired manner. It may be only a coincidence, but four of them had been nurses—a vocation that trained them in the care of other human beings—and they had enjoyed their careers before willingly giving them up to raise their families.

For me, though, almost everything I do for my children is a chore. This pains me because I love them and should *want* to give myself freely to them. One day before the school term began, I took them to lunch. I had selected a restaurant I thought they would both enjoy. We went shopping first and then to the park before reaching the restaurant. They were so proud and seemed to feel very grown up. Yet I didn't enjoy myself. I was nice to them, I chatted with them, I tried to make them feel at home—and yet I couldn't wait for us to finish up and leave so I could go home and do whatever it was that might give me more pleasure that day. Glancing around the restaurant, I saw several mothers lunching with their children. They all seemed to be enjoying it. I asked myself what in God's name was wrong with me—I must be the only woman in the place not enjoying the experience. But now I wonder if I didn't look the same way to them as they did to me and if perhaps many of them (if not all) didn't feel the same.

I strongly urge all mothers to be honest with themselves, their families, and each other—and with their sons and daughters and other young people when they arrive at the threshold of parenthood. The next time you feel an impulse to ask a childless couple when they are going to start their family, don't. Check that compulsion to talk about the boundless joys of motherhood and boast about your own children unless you honestly temper your words with the negatives. Don't tell a carefree, child-free young wife that she'll never know the delight of having a small child present her with a Mother's Day gift unless you also tell her she'll also never know how dreadful it is to sit up all night with a feverish child.

To young women who have not yet taken that irreversible step of motherhood, I want to offer my closing words.

There are at least two ways of dealing with the subtle bullying that those who elect to remain childless have to put up with. The first is a very loud "MIND YOUR OWN BUSINESS!" People who try to manipulate you into having children are being rude, crude, and thoughtless. It's no one's business if your ovaries aren't functioning—and no one's business if they are. You don't need to justify a decision not to have children—to anyone. You are entitled, indeed you are obliged, to make your own judgments in these matters, and unless those urging you to have children are also willing to finance the venture and help you take care of the products of their busybodying, you don't owe them even a polite answer.

If, however, you feel obligated to answer in some way, you might try asking a question of your own. Something warm and personal, like: "Have you ever thought about having your face lifted?" or perhaps: "Where did you ever get that interesting wart?"

If you are being pressured by friends or relatives to "prove yourself" or feel on the verge of succumbing to the persuasion of the media, consider the advice of one who has been there: The attention I received during both my pregnancies was enough to convince anyone that mothers are loved by all, and hence their children will be welcomed with open arms. When I gave birth, I had no peace because of the constant phone calls and visitors, and I received something like nineteen floral arrangements and innumerable gifts while I was in the hospital. But after the fanfare of the first year or so, I learned that the very people who apply the pressure to bear and provide the initial attention tend to shy away once the babies become nuisances, and you may find yourself a social reject by the very folks who pitied your childless state.

If you don't want children or are not certain that you are ready to have them, stick to your guns. It makes no sense to enter into a lifetime contract making you responsible for another human being for the singular reason of pleasing or pacifying someone else who will bear no responsibility for the child you are being urged to have.

Parenthood is tough. For some mothers, it wrings all the joy out of their lives. For them, Mother's Day, as a day to rejoice, is truly over.

AUTHOR'S NOTE

In the course of being a mother, I've learned what it's like to feel what other parents feel—the overwhelming responsibility for the health and welfare of two other human beings, the intense and special love that a mother knows, and how confusing and devastating it is to have these weighty feelings periodically combined with feelings of rage and hostility.

And in the course of putting it into words I wondered why it was that thus far I'd been able to keep my periodic rage under control. I decided to look more carefully at parents who weren't so fortunate. Looking back, I truly believe that I was so motivated because I was fearful that one day I wouldn't be able to maintain control and would hurt one of the people I love the very most. In any case, this led to a good deal of research—so far about three years' worth—into the phenomenon of child abuse. Because I'm a mother I understand at a very gut level what's behind the forces that drive many loving parents over the brink and find to their horror that what started out as anger or honest discipline has turned into full-scale violence. I also understand how a parent can be so filled with resentment that he or she falls into a pattern of nagging and insulting a child to such an extent that it can only be labeled emotional abuse. The tragic result can be an injured child and an emotionally damaged family.

I've learned too that even when the situation doesn't reach this point, many parents harbor the fear that it might, and they feel very much alone. Who can they tell "I'm afraid I'm going to lose my temper and kill my child?" Who too, can they talk to about the odd combination of emotions that coexist on a nearly daily basis? And so many parents, whether they are potentially abusive or simply fearful that they are inadequate to the task of rearing their children feel they have no one to talk to, no way to relieve the

233

pressure: they work alternately to control these feelings or deny their existence. So parental stress builds up.

Often making matters worse, is that many young mothers have no time away from their children—no time to collect their thoughts or have a much needed rest. And even those mothers who *are* able to leave their children with a sitter or a friend can experience times of emotional crisis and that they must get away—and at that very moment. But because crisis can't be scheduled with the appropriate arrangements for child care made in advance, no relief is in sight when it's needed the most.

My investigation into parental stress and child abuse led me to the discovery of several self-help organizations that have sprung up across the nation: Parents Anonymous (a national organization) Families Anonymous in Denver, Child Abuse Listening Mediation (CALM) in Santa Barbara, Parental Stress Service in Berkeley, to name just a few. These groups work to alleviate parental stress and prevent the emotional and physical abuse of children before it happens by providing a 24-hour telephone hotline for troubled parents. Callers are assured confidentiality, friendship, understanding, and the freedom to let off steam. All of these organizations maintain listings of agencies and professionals for parents who need more than a sympathetic ear. They hold group meetings where parents can get together and help one another work through their conflicts; some of the groups are led by professionals, some by lay therapists, and some by other parents who've worked through their own problems. CALM provides homemaking services for overwhelmed parents, Parental Stress Service provides respite child care, and all of them provide help and friendship.

After corresponding and visiting with some of the people who've made these groups possible, I became truly inspired by the stories they had to tell. Instead of being depressed by hearing about a whole string of tragedies and how very overwhelmed and depressed so many parents are, I heard hundreds of stories about parents who have learned to reverse their destructive patterns and find joy in their lives. Thousands of people, over the years, have gotten help— when they thought they had nowhere to turn—by lifting up the telephone.

At the same time I was learning about the self-help groups, I was averaging three speeches each week to groups of mothers. In the groups I found—just as I had when I was writing the book and talking openly with other mothers —that honesty begets honesty: Often it was as if many of the mothers at these meetings had been waiting for the opportunity to unburden themselves. Instead of hearing a scant 200 tales of frustration and unhappiness, I was hearing thousands of them. And women were asking me for help. I looked around to see what services were available in the community and found them wanting.

I suppose it was inevitable, probably from the first time I heard about the first group, that I'd be pushed into putting my organizational skills to work. With the help of several other women who shared my feelings, I organized a telephone hotline service here in Palo Alto (and subsequently showed other women in other communities how to do the same thing). Our service offers a telephone hotline, respite child care, and friendship when it's needed to carry parents through stressful times. We maintain a complete referral service of what's available in the community and have an advisory board composed of psychologists, pediatricians, and other trained professionals. The hotline is staffed by 22 empathetic and fully trained volunteers, most of whom are parents.

The hotline now receives an average of five telephone calls each day and they last anywhere from twenty minutes to an hour and a half; we've had suicide calls, calls from mothers who beat their children, calls from mothers who fear they are going insane, and calls from mothers who are so guilt ridden by what they see as their inadequacies that they are in deep depressions. Some of our callers call only once, some every week, and some every day. Some of them want us to call them periodically to see how they're doing— and when we do they say they know someone cares about them. And away from the line, our volunteers have been told by friends, neighbors, and even casual acquaintances that just knowing the hotline is there should they ever need it is reassuring, even though they may never place a call.

Our dream is to establish a 24-hour drop-in center to provide crisis baby sitting for parents in trouble, a place

235

where parents can meet and talk to other parents, and a place where much needed friendships can develop.

Much more is needed, but the parent groups and hotlines are a start. Right alongside our dream for a center is the dream that there will be just this—the start—in all cities and communities across the nation. To this end, we've formed a non-profit corporation to educate the general public about the problems of abuse and to serve as a vehicle to help other concerned citizens form hotline groups in their own communities. Because we feel that the quality of life for every parent and child is the concern of us all, we've called our organization

QUALITY OF LIFE
220 Miramonte Ave.
Palo Alto, Calif., 94306

and anyone who might want more information need only drop us a line.

Shirley L. Radl
November, 1974

NOTES

Chapter 1: A Mother Is

1. E. James Lieberman, "Informed Consent for Parenthood," *Abortion and the Unwanted Children,* California Committee on Therapeutic Abortion, Springer Publishing Co., New York, 1971.
2. Report of the Commission on Population Growth and the American Future, New American Library, New York, 1972, p. 126.

Chapter 3: The Garden of Eden

1. Niles Newton, *The Family Book of Child Care,* Harper & Brothers, New York, 1957.
2. Ibid.

Chapter 6: School Days

1. Joseph and Lois Bird, *Power to the Parents,* Doubleday, New York, 1972.
2. John Holt, *Freedom and Beyond,* Dutton, New York, 1972.

Chapter 8: Spare the Rod

1. Benjamin Spock, *Baby and Child Care,* Pocket Books (revised edition), New York, 1968.
2. Haim Ginott, *Between Parent and Child,* Macmillan, New York, 1965.
3. Ibid.
4. Edward Edelson, "It's the Parent Who Needs Help," *Family Health,* July 1971.
5. Vincent J. Fontana, "Which Parents Abuse Children?" *Medical Insight,* October 1971.
6. *Time,* November 7, 1969.
7. Carol Schneider, Carl Pollock, and Ray E. Helfer, "Interviewing the Parents," Chapter 4 of *Helping the Battered*

Child and His Family, edited by C. Henry Kempe and Roy E. Helfer, Lippincott, 1972.

Chapter 9: Marital Bliss and Children
1. Ellen Peck, "The Media and Maternity—Some Problem Areas"; statement presented to the Senate Labor and Public Welfare Committee, Subcommittee on Human Resources, October 5, 1971, Washington D.C.
2. E. E. Masters, "Parenthood as Crises," *Marriages and Family Living*, vol. 19, no. 4, November 1957.
3. Arthur P. Jacoby, *Journal of Marriage and the Family*, November 1969.
4. Harold Feldman, "Changes and Parenthood: A Methodological Design," unpublished study, Cornell University, Ithaca, New York.
5. Anna and Arnold Silverman, *The Case Against Having Children*, David McKay Co., New York, 1971.
6. Jack Harrison Pollack, "Why Marriages Break Up After Forty," *Family Health*, July 1972.

Chapter 11: They Are Worth Their Weight In Gold
1. *Report of the President's Commission on Population Growth and the American Future*, New American Library, New York, 1972.
2. Ellen Peck, *The Baby Trap*, Bernard Geis Associates, New York, 1971.

Chapter 12: Doctor, Lawyer, Indian Chief . . .
or Mother?
1. William V. Shannon, *The New York Times Magazine*, April 30, 1972.
2. Benjamin Spock, *Baby and Child Care*, Pocket Books (revised edition), New York, 1968.

ABOUT THE AUTHOR

Shirley L. Radl has been active in community affairs and politics and presently serves as an alternate delegate to the California State Democratic Central Committee. Her articles have appeared in *Life, Cosmopolitan, Environmental Quality Magazine,* and *Population, Environment and People* (McGraw-Hill).

Born and raised in California, Ms. Radl attended San Jose State College. She lives in Palo Alto, California, with her husband and two children.